973
.523
0924
Brown

Latham, Frank Brown, 1910–
　　Jacob Brown and the War of 1812, by Frank B. Latham.
[1st ed.]　New York, Cowles Book Co. [1971]

　　x, 161 p.　illus., maps, ports.　22 cm.　$4.95

　　A biography of the Quaker schoolteacher who became one of the prominent military leaders of the American forces in the War of 1812.
　　Bibliography: p. [151]

RELATED
BOOKS IN
CATALOG
UNDER

　　1. Brown, Jacob, 1775–1828.　2. U. S.—History—War of 1812.
[1. Brown, Jacob, 1775–1828. 2. U. S.—History—War of 1812]　I.
Title.

E353.1.B9L3　1971

87794

70–144121

973.5'23'0924　[B]　[92]

ISBN 0-402-14006-0

MARC

JACOB BROWN
and the
WAR of 1812

JACOB BROWN
and the
WAR of 1812

By FRANK B. LATHAM

COWLES BOOK COMPANY, INC.
NEW YORK

For Lucille and Linda

Contents

Introduction

May 29, 1813. The War of 1812 had been dragging on for months, and American armies along the Canadian border had blundered into one defeat after another. Now, a strong British force commanded by Sir George Prevost was preparing to land and attack Sackets Harbor, New York. This port on Lake Ontario was the United States' one good base of operations on the Great Lakes. Prevost had over 1,000 well-trained British and Canadian troops. Opposing him were 500 untrained New York militia and 400 American regulars, many of them ill, commanded by Colonel Electus Backus. Fortunately for the United States, this American force was commanded by Brigadier General Jacob Brown of the New York militia.

At that time, no one knew how fortunate the nation was in having a man like Brown. Surely, few people expected that he had much military ability. Brown was a Pennsylvania Quaker, a former schoolteacher and surveyor. He had bought land near Watertown, New York, and established a village called Brownville. Brown prospered and in 1809 was appointed colonel of the local militia. He was a handsome, friendly man whose comfortable house was a good place for the militia to hold pleasant get-togethers.

As Brown's political influence grew, Governor Daniel Tompkins of New York appointed him brigadier general of the militia. At that time, Brown had had no experience leading men into action. In fact, he knew next to nothing about military drill and tactics.

When the war began, Brown had showed considerable energy in defending Ogdensburg, New York. But that was all the service he saw until May of 1813, when he called out his militia to help Colonel Backus defend Sackets Harbor.

Brown's pick-up force gave the British a sound beating, and Sackets Harbor was saved. It was a small battle but a vital victory. Loss of this port might well have cost the nation its whole northern frontier. It was through Sackets Harbor that most of the supplies went to Oliver Hazard Perry, whose fleet won the all-important Battle of Lake Erie, September 10, 1813. Perry's success cleared the way for General William Henry Harrison's sweep into Canada and his victory over the British and Indians at the Battle of the Thames on October 5 of that year.

Jacob Brown was by birth and training a man of peace. But when his country went to war, he became a fighting man. The great military historian, Admiral A. T. Mahan, wrote of Brown: "Barring the single exception of the Battle of New Orleans, his career on the Niagara peninsula is the one operation of the land war of 1812 upon which thoughtful Americans of the following generations could look back with satisfaction."

JACOB BROWN
and the
WAR of 1812

1

LURE OF THE WEST

Jacob Brown was born in Bucks County, Pennsylvania, on May 9, 1775, less than a month after the Battle of Lexington. His ancestors had for several generations been members of the Society of Friends (Quakers). Samuel Brown, Jacob's father, was a prosperous farmer. But he plunged into commercial ventures, gambling on a rise in prices, and lost all of his property when Jacob was 16 years old. After that, young Brown worked at any job he could find, and studied at night. His education was said to have been "accurate and useful, as far as it went." When he was 18, Jacob got a job teaching school in Crosswicks, New Jersey, where he remained for two years.

At this time, the tide of emigration was beginning to flow westward to Ohio, and Jacob decided to try his luck in a new land. He went to Cincinnati and obtained a post as surveyor on the public lands. In 1798, Brown went back east and taught at the Friends School in New York City. The newspapers there were full of heated discussions of French-American relations. The French government had accused the United

States of pro-British behavior and had set French ships to harassing and capturing American merchant vessels.

In the spring of 1798, Congress authorized American merchant ships to "repel by force any assault," and ordered the navy to seize armed French ships that were hunting down American vessels. Later, American frigates whipped the French in three naval battles in the Caribbean area.

When a full-fledged war with France threatened, ex-President George Washington, who had been named commanding general of the army, appointed Alexander Hamilton to the rank of major general in July 1798. Hamilton spent several months in New York raising troops for operations in Florida and Louisiana. Meanwhile, Brown had written several newspaper articles discussing the quarrel with France. Hamilton read the articles, was impressed by Brown's keen mind and level head, and appointed Brown his military secretary. As Hamilton's secretary, Brown had little chance to learn anything about military drill or tactics. But he did see at first hand the problems of supplying and organizing an army—problems he was later to face and solve during the War of 1812. The brilliant Hamilton, an officer during the Revolution, and ex-secretary of the treasury, encouraged Brown to study law.

President John Adams cut short Hamilton's war preparations by sending peace commissioners to meet with Napoleon in Paris. Being already involved in a war with Britain, Napoleon was ready to talk peace. The Convention of 1800 finally brought the undeclared war with France to an end.

While the peace talks with France dragged on, Brown kept busy studying law, but he dropped it after a few months. His experience in Ohio was fresh in his mind, and he still dreamed of making a success of business or farming in the new lands to the west.

Brown's chance to move west again came when he met

the general agent of a land company who persuaded Brown to purchase several thousand acres of wilderness land near Lake Ontario in western New York, and to become the agent in charge of starting a settlement there. Frontier land was cheap, and Brown was able to scrape up enough money to make the purchase. Then, with four hired men, Brown traveled west and began clearing land near Philomel Creek on the Black River, Jefferson County, in March of 1799. His father's family left Bucks County and joined him in May.

In the fall of 1800, Brown built a mill at the mouth of Philomel Creek. In 1801, he built a grist mill. The next year, Brown, now a prosperous landowner and farmer, married Pamelia Williams. A generous, outgoing man, he took a personal interest in the problems of his neighbors and the tenants on his land. His wife, Pamelia, was an efficient housekeeper who became a prudent manager of her husband's business affairs during his long absences from home in 1813 and 1814.

By September 1805, the settlement of Brownville contained 25 houses. The grist mill and a store were owned by Jacob and his father, Samuel. Later, Jacob's brother took charge of the store. As the leading man of his community, Brown won the attention of Governor Daniel Tompkins, who appointed him colonel and later brigadier general of the state militia.

News of the United States' long-drawn-out quarrel with Britain began to stir up the busy settlers in faraway Brownville. Brown's Quaker beliefs had by now been changed somewhat by world conditions, and he reluctantly felt the nation soon would have to take a stand. In a letter to Governor Tompkins in 1811, Brown wrote: "I am not one of those that believes war with Great Britain the best thing that can happen to my country. But to my humble vision, it appears that we must fight or cease to prate about national sovereignty, and national honor and dignity." He added, "I am serious in my application to be on duty if there be war."

A brief review of the United States' efforts to protect its rights in a world swept by war will explain why Brown, a man of peace, finally chose to fight.

2

DRIFT TO WAR

The young United States had, from the beginning of its history, sought to keep clear of Europe's quarrels and wars. President Washington had trouble with Britain and France, but managed to avoid taking sides in their conflicts and remained neutral. Jay's Treaty of 1794 settled most British-American differences, but it angered France. President John Adams, who took office in 1797, ignored the hotheads in his pro-British Federalist party and worked hard for peace. The Convention of 1800 ended the trouble with France but led to Adams's defeat in the 1800 election by Thomas Jefferson and his Republicans. (The Republicans were later called Democratic-Republicans and finally Democrats in the 1820's.)

In 1802, Jefferson's second year in the presidency, Napoleon signed a peace treaty with Britain. But war broke out again in 1803, and American trade began to suffer. Jefferson tried to protect American rights by discussions and economic coercion (refusing to trade with any nation that interfered with our merchants), but without much success. Caught between Britain and France, the United States could not trade with the nations of Europe without running into rules that these two nations had adopted to cripple one another.

Britain, which looked upon Napoleon's empire as a threat to the world of free men, felt that the United States should be willing to cooperate until France was beaten. The British were in no mood to listen to the Americans' talk about a country's "right" to trade wherever it pleased. Britain insisted on the right to stop any merchant ship that might be carrying goods to a French port. The United States contended that only contraband, goods that directly aided the French war effort, could be seized. Britain took the attitude that almost any product shipped to France could aid its war effort. The United States stubbornly insisted that "free ships make free goods."

Aside from searching for contraband, British ship captains also were on the lookout for deserters from the Royal Navy. Because of the hard work, harsh discipline, low pay, and poor food, thousands of British sailors deserted in those days. Many of them joined the U.S. Navy or signed on with American merchant ships, where the pay, food, and working conditions were better. British captains, hard pressed to get men for their ships, impressed English as well as foreign sailors (the seizure of men for service in the navy). "Press" gangs seized men in British seaports or took them off merchant ships. A British sailor who wanted the protection of the American flag could do so by taking out naturalization papers. But the British insisted on the principle of "once an Englishman always an Englishman."

Britain did not claim the right to impress native-born Americans, though. But British captains, desperate for men, were likely to make "mistakes," which took the British government months or years to correct. The United States looked upon impressment as barbaric and an insult to an independent country.

The pressure on the United States was increased in 1806 by an Order-in-Council issued by the British government which placed a strict blockade on much of the European coast. Napoleon struck back with the Berlin Decree. It declared the British Isles in a state of blockade; no vessel coming from or touching a British port would be allowed to enter any port controlled by France.

During 1807, British-American relations reached a point near war. On June 22, the U.S. frigate *Chesapeake* sailed from Norfolk, Virginia. When she was 10 miles at sea, she was stopped by the British frigate *Leopard*. The British captain demanded the right to search the American frigate for deserters. Commodore James Barron refused, and the *Leopard* then fired broadsides into the *Chesapeake* for 10 minutes, killing three men and wounding 18. When Barron hauled down his flag, a British boarding party took four sailors, allegedly deserters.

The *Chesapeake* limped back to Norfolk, followed by the *Leopard,* which anchored near the American frigate and behaved as if nothing important had happened. But the *Chesapeake*'s report of the action sent waves of anger through the country and many people demanded war. Young Winfield Scott was among those ready for action. He gave up the practice of law and joined the army. John Quincy Adams, son of ex-President Adams, left the Federalist party when he heard a Federalist speaker defend the actions of the *Leopard*.

President Jefferson promptly issued a proclamation prohibiting British ships from entering American ports to take on supplies. But he wanted to cool the war fever while using the *Leopard* affair to gain a settlement of American grievances with Britain. The United States demanded the return of the seamen taken from the *Chesapeake* and also insisted that the British stop impressing men from American vessels. Britain replied that it had never claimed the right to search vessels of the U.S. Navy. In return, it offered money to the wounded and the families of the dead. Payment finally was made, but it was long in coming. The *Leopard* affair poisoned British-American relations for several years.

British and French seizures of American merchant ships increased, and Jefferson tried a startling new idea. In December 1807, he persuaded Congress to approve the Embargo Act, which forbade American ships to sail to any foreign port. Jefferson felt that Britain and France would be more willing to respect American rights when they no longer could buy American wheat, cotton, or tobacco. He called his daring new policy "peaceable coercion."

The embargo hit Southern planters hard, however. Cotton and tobacco prices plunged, and surpluses piled up in warehouses. The seaport towns of New England were crowded with idle ships and starving sailors. Shipowners protested loudly that they wanted no protection for their vessels. They were willing to take their chances. They contended that if one ship in three escaped capture, they could still make a big profit because of the high prices paid for American goods in Europe.

Jefferson refused to retreat, and he was supported by a majority of his party, particularly the settlers beyond the Ohio River. In this area, which was rapidly filling with people, the British and the Canadians were accused of stirring up trouble between the Indians and the Americans. The settlers in the Northwest declared that the Indians were being generously supplied with arms to attack isolated villages. They wanted to end this menace by taking Canada away from Britain. Furthermore, they wanted a free outlet to the sea down the St. Lawrence River. The Embargo Act looked to the settlers as if it might lead to war, and that would be all right with them.

John Quincy Adams was among the senators who voted for the Embargo Act. The Massachusetts voters were outraged. Nine months before his term as senator expired, the Federalist-controlled state legislature elected Adams's successor. (Not until 1914 were senators directly elected by the people.) Considering this an insult, Adams resigned.

"Embargo breakers" were soon busy making money. They sailed at night from remote bays and creeks. Britain encouraged them by allowing American ships to enter British ports without clearance papers. There also was a large illegal trade across the Canadian border, which later hampered the American war effort against the British.

Despite its bad effects on the South, the embargo gave American industry a big boost because it created a scarcity of foreign-made goods. Throughout the North, factories began to hum, and farmers who could not sell their crops crowded into towns to work in factories and mills. Ironically, Jefferson, who hated cities and factories, promoted their growth by trying to avoid the war. The agricultural South, which Jefferson favored, was impoverished while New England prospered. Industry became more important than commerce.

After a year in which the nation was brought close to civil war, Congress voted to repeal the Embargo Act, and Jefferson signed the bill on March 1, 1809, without comment. In place of the Embargo Act, Congress substituted an act of non-intercourse. It forbade Americans to trade with Britain and France, but permitted trade with the rest of the world. Three days after the Embargo Act was repealed, Jefferson's second term ended. He was succeeded by his close friend, James Madison.

The Non-Intercourse Act proved no more effective than had the Embargo Act, and relations with Britain in particular continued to go downhill. Helping them to deteriorate were the actions of the new British minister to the United States, Francis James Jackson. The insolent Jackson soon had Americans in an uproar. One of his contributions to British-American relations was to call President Madison "a plain and rather mean-looking little man." Jackson also said that all Americans were alike "except that a few are less knaves than others." The U.S. government soon asked Britain to call Jackson home.

For a year after Jackson was recalled, Britain did nothing about sending a minister to replace him. British policy during this period was as fumbling as was American policy. Britain knew that nothing could be gained and much might be lost in a war with the United States. The bitter, life-and-death struggle with Napoleon had put a heavy strain on Britain. Its foreign trade had fallen drastically. Wheat was selling at four dollars a bushel on the grain markets (a very high price in those days), and British workers were near starvation.

The British government wanted peace with the United States, but at the same time its Orders-in-Council were still in force, and British warships were still seizing American ships. In the Great Lakes region, an Indian war had flared up, and captured Indians were found to be well supplied with British guns. The great Indian chief, Tecumseh, was finally beaten by General William Henry Harrison at the Battle of Tippecanoe, but despite their defeat the Indians remained a threat. The settlers believed that Britain, the supporter of the Indians, was the foe who should be fought.

In the spring of 1811, two British frigates, the *Guerrière* and the *Melampus,* loitered insolently outside New York harbor, stopping American ships and impressing seamen. On May 16, Commodore John Rodgers of the U.S. frigate *President* sighted a ship he thought to be the *Guerrière*. There was a confused exchange of hails in the gathering darkness, and the ships began shooting. After a 45-minute exchange of fire, the British ship ran away. She turned out to be the *Little Belt,* a 20-gun sloop of war, and nine of her crew were killed and 23 wounded. Americans recalled the *Leopard* affair and decided that this had evened the score. No apologies were offered by the U.S. government. War fever was rising in America.

While the nation was still cheering the *President*'s chastizing of *Little Belt,* a new British minister, Augustus John Foster, arrived. He was authorized to make payments to the victims of the *Leopard* affair, but to make no other concessions to the United States. Foster's talks with President Madison and Secretary of State James Monroe convinced the Americans that the United States had but two choices: give in to the British or fight. President Madison tired of talking and escaped the heat of Washington by going to his home, Montpelier, Virginia. Before he left, he issued a proclamation calling Congress into session in November instead of December.

The new Congress that met in November 1811 was really *new.* The elections of 1810 had resulted in the defeat of nearly half of the old congressmen. Among the new members were a vigorous anti-British group of young Republicans from the South and West. They were led by 34-year-old Henry Clay of Kentucky. He had served two terms in the Senate, and was chosen Speaker of the House on the day he was sworn in as a member. Clay's followers were called "War Hawks" by the Federalists, who accused them of wanting to rush the nation into a war.

Clay rallied his followers by blithely declaring that "the militia of Kentucky alone are competent to place Montreal and Upper Canada at your feet." John C. Calhoun, 29-year-old South Carolina War Hawk, said, "I believe that in four weeks from the time a declaration of war is heard on our frontier, the whole of Upper Canada [now Ontario] and part of Lower Canada [Quebec] will be in our power."

Historian Edward Channing said that ". . . in advocating conquest, the Westerners were not actuated merely by desire for land; they welcomed war because they thought it would be the easiest way to abate Indian troubles. The savages were supported by the fur-trading interests that centered at Quebec and London."

President Madison's message to Congress did not please the War Hawks. He recounted Britain's misdeeds over the years, but he issued no call for action *now* against that nation. He did, however, indicate a willingness to approve stronger measures in order to force a change in British policies. He left things up to Clay and his men, and they were not slow about acting.

The Republican-controlled Congress adopted a series of resolutions denouncing Britain's interference with American trade, the impressment of seamen, and the supplying of arms to the Indians. They also recommended adding 10,000 men to the regular army, calling for 50,000 volunteers (militia) from the states, arming merchant ships, and overhauling and outfitting existing warships. Nothing more was done about building up the navy, which had only six frigates, three sloops of war, and seven smaller ships. Even some of the fieriest War Hawks felt it was no use for the navy to try to challenge Britain, the greatest naval power in the world.

Some members of the Federalist party, which was slowly dying, voted for the War Hawk resolutions. (It was a purely political move by the generally pro-British Federalists.) They believed that if the United States went to war, it would take a beating and the Republicans would lose the next election. Then the Federalists would regain control of Congress and make peace.

When Congress was asked to vote to increase the army by 10,000 men, the Federalists and some anti-war Republicans sought to embarrass the President. They proposed a 25,000-man increase, knowing the nation could not afford such a large army. But the War Hawks called their bluff and voted for the bill. It became a law in January 1812, and the size of the army was increased—at least on paper—to 35,000 men.

Then Congress took up the bill authorizing the President to call for the 50,000 volunteers, to be commanded by officers appointed by state officials. These men were to be ordered into the service when the President decided that they were needed. This brought up a knotty question. Did the President have the power under the Constitution to send the state militia outside the boundaries of the United States? Critics said the Constitution provided that Congress might call out the militia "to suppress insurrections and repel invasions," but didn't say clearly that state militia could be ordered to invade another country. When the militia bill finally passed, Congress had ignored the question. But later it caused a lot of trouble when the militia was called into service.

Still looking for ways to avoid military conflict, Federalists and anti-war Republicans hoped that news of American preparations for war would cause Britain to soften her attitude. But their hopes were shattered in May 1812, when dispatches from Britain arrived. The British government merely repeated that it could not repeal its Orders-in-Council so long as France had not repealed its decrees against American trade. It was "the insidious policy of the enemy," said Britain, that was causing all the trouble, and the United States had no right to complain about British policies.

This apparently final refusal of Britain to soften its policy brought action by President Madison. He submitted his war message to Congress on June 1. The message charged Britain with: encouraging Indians to attack American settlers; impressing American sailors; letting British warships lurk near American ports and harass American ships; injuring American trade by the blockade and the Orders-in-Council.

Congress completed action on the declaration of war by June 17, and the President signed it the next day. Five days after the declaration of war, Britain removed one of the main causes of the conflict by repealing the Orders-in-Council. Repeal had been brought about not by American threats but by the severe depression that had gripped Britain for two years. All ports in western Europe, except those of Portugal, had been closed to British ships by Napoleon's armies. The Non-Intercourse Act had shut off the American market. So British goods had piled up in warehouses, and factories closed one by one. The price of bread had skyrocketed, and workers were rioting. Merchants, who feared the permanent loss of markets through the growth of American manufacturing, brought strong pressure for repeal of the orders. Finally on June 22 they were repealed, but there was no way that this news could have reached the United States before Congress declared war.

Almost immediately after war was declared, efforts were made to patch up a quick peace. The British thought their repeal of the orders would bring a quick agreement. But the U.S. government still demanded that Britain give up the practice of impressing seamen. The British hinted that they would reduce search and impressment to a minimum for American ships, but they refused to surrender the principle.

New England shipowners angrily insisted that search and impressment were not important. But the men of the South and West, which had neither ships nor sailors, filled the newspapers with the slogan: "Free trade and sailors' rights." They insisted that no country that allowed its ships to be stopped and searched could claim to be independent. Westerners also were infuriated by the New Englanders' airy dismissal of British-inspired Indian raids as being unimportant. So, to an extent, the nation went to war to defend the rights of New Englanders whether they wanted them defended or not.

3

DISASTER IN THE WEST

When the war began, the regular army actually totaled less than 7,000 men. Only seven infantry regiments, two artillery regiments, and one dragoon regiment (heavily armed cavalry) had received enough training to be reasonably efficient fighting outfits. In preparing for war, Congress had voted to increase the army to 35,000 men, but had neglected to provide money to recruit and equip them. Congress finally stirred itself and provided enlistment bounties of $40 a man for regular army recruits, plus three months' pay in advance and 160 acres of land. But despite these rewards, the army grew to only about 15,000 by the end of 1812.

In selecting men to lead the army, President Madison had to choose between young men with little or no military experience and aged veterans of the Revolutionary War. Unfortunately, he picked the veterans. His two major generals were Henry Dearborn, ex-secretary of war, and Thomas Pinckney of South Carolina. The average age of the generals selected was 60 years. Only 71 graduates of the U.S. Military Academy at West Point were available for duty. The Academy, which had been reluctantly founded by President Jefferson in 1802, was described as "a puny, rickety child." Jefferson and his Republicans were suspicious of a strong army and had put their faith in state militia. They rather regretted that the Academy had been established and gave it little support. President Madison appeared to feel the same way, and as late as September 1812, with a war on, only one professor and one cadet were at West Point.

The small regular army, which already had plenty of problems, was further burdened by Secretary of War William Eustis. He was a penny-pincher who was more interested in saving money than in buying the supplies needed by the army.

President Madison correctly decided that an immediate attack should be made on Montreal in Lower Canada. Seizure of this city would cut British communications on the St. Lawrence River with Upper Canada to the west, and would keep the enemy from invading the Ohio Valley. Since the small regular army was scattered in forts throughout the country, the only way to strike quickly at Montreal was to call on the New England militia. But when President Madison asked for troops from Massachusetts, Governor Caleb Strong refused to comply. The governor of Connecticut also refused to send troops on the ground that his state was not being invaded. Because of the bitter opposition to "Mr. Madison's war," most of the militia in the New England states never was called into service during the war.

Since the governors of Massachusetts and Connecticut refused to cooperate with him, President Madison had to come up with another campaign plan. This one called for a two-pronged attack on Upper Canada from Detroit on the west and the Niagara River on the east. This was a poor substitute for an attack on Montreal, but everyone was eager to get on with the war, so the invasion of Upper Canada was approved by Madison's advisers.

General William Hull, a 60-year-old veteran of the Revolutionary War, was ordered to march from Dayton, Ohio,
to Detroit and take command of the army in the Northwest.
Secretary of War Eustis, still hunting for bargains in army
supplies, took time out long enough to write Hull's orders. But
although these orders were dated June 18, the day war was
declared, Eustis neglected to tell Hull that the war was on. To
speed up his march through very rough country, Hull decided
to ship much of his equipment to Detroit on a schooner. To
reach Detroit, the ship had to sail past Fort Malden, a British
post on the Canadian side of the Detroit River. There, she was
captured by a British warship, whose captain knew that war
had been declared. The British commander at Fort Malden
got this news on June 27, six days before it reached Hull. Of
course, Hull should have been more cautious. He knew that
he was not being sent to Detroit just to see what the country
looked like. But this blunder was just one of several he made
during the Detroit campaign.

Hull reached Detroit on July 5 and entered Upper Canada on July 12. Instead of immediately attacking Fort Malden,
which was weakly defended, Hull occupied Sandwich, right
across the river from Detroit, and started worrying about what
would happen if the Indians attacked his supply line. On July
17, a small British force captured the American post at Michili-
mackinac in northern Michigan. This setback caused Hull to
retreat to Detroit. Then he sent word for the commander at
Fort Dearborn (now Chicago) to come to his aid. But the
Indians captured Fort Dearborn and killed most of the garrison.

Then, the brilliant General Isaac Brock, British commander in Upper Canada, scraped up a few British regulars
(there were only 5,000 in all of Canada) and hurried to Detroit. Brock bamboozled Hull by dressing Canadian militia
in the red coats of British troops and parading them in sight
of the American lines. He also hinted to the shaken Hull that

it might be difficult for the British to control their Indian allies during an attack. Hull lost his nerve and surrendered his army on August 16, 1812.

A few days before Boston received the news of General Hull's cowardly surrender at Detroit, the U.S. frigate *Constitution* had sailed into Boston harbor with prisoners from the British frigate *Guerrière*. The *Constitution,* commanded by Captain Isaac Hull, nephew of General Hull, had shot the British ship to pieces in a two-hour duel. This victory kept the spirits of Americans from touching bottom when the loss of Detroit was confirmed. Historian Henry Adams wrote: "Isaac Hull was nephew to the unhappy General and perhaps the shattered hulk of the *Guerrière,* which the nephew left at the bottom of the Atlantic Ocean . . . was worth, for the moment, the whole province which the uncle had lost."

Even the grumpy, anti-war New Englanders led the cheers for Captain Hull and his men. After all, the *Constitution* had been built in Boston and most of her crew were New England men. Hull's victory set the *Times* of London to mourning that "never before in the history of the world did an English frigate strike [surrender] to an American." The *Times* feared that this victory would make the Americans "insolent and confident." And later news from the sea frontier bore out the *Times*'s prediction.

On October 25, the frigate *United States,* commanded by Captain Stephen Decatur, hammered the British frigate *Macedonian* into submission. On December 29, the *Constitution,* now commanded by Captain William Bainbridge and later known proudly as "Old Ironsides," brushed off the shots of the British frigate *Java* and sank her near the coast of South America.

Smaller American ships also were busy "twisting the British lion's tail." On October 17, the *Wasp,* an 18-gun sloop of war commanded by Captain Jacob Jones, smashed the *Frolic*. In February 1813, the *Hornet,* commanded by Captain James Lawrence, beat the *Peacock*. During the sea war, the American navy won seven out of eight small-ship actions. During the war, the largest American ships in action were frigates, carrying 44 to 54 guns. Sloops of war and brigs carried from 18 to 20 guns. Schooners, which were used on the Great Lakes and on Lake Champlain, had eight to twelve guns. Besides frigates, sloops of war, and brigs, the British used battleships, which carried from 74 to 110 guns.

American naval victories would never have been won if the plan of President Madison and his advisers had been followed. They believed that it was no use for the small American navy to challenge British naval power. Therefore, they decided that all American ships should be kept safe in port to serve as floating gun platforms for the defense of the harbors. Captains William Bainbridge and Charles Stewart heard of this plan and protested violently to President Madison. They convinced him to let American captains go out and seek the enemy. "Eight times out of ten, Sir," said Captain Stewart, "with equal force, we can hardly fail. We may be captured and probably shall, because their numbers are greater than ours. But the American flag will never be dishonored, seldom, if ever, struck [surrendered] to equal force."

Aroused by the American victories, in early 1813 Britain sent strong naval forces to blockade the American coast. As a result, most of the American warships were bottled up in ports for the rest of the war. But in June 1813, Captain Lawrence, commanding the hard-luck frigate *Chesapeake,* which had been mauled by *Leopard,* unwisely accepted the challenge of Captain Philip B. V. Broke of the *Shannon*. Lawrence had had little time to train his green crew, while Broke had drilled his men for months. After a savage battle, the *Chesapeake* was captured, but the words of the dying Lawrence became a motto of the United States Navy: "Don't give up the ship."

Within a week after Hull's surrender at Detroit, the energetic General Isaac Brock was back at the Niagara frontier preparing to repel a force of U.S. regulars and New York state militia, the second part of Madison's two-pronged attack. On October 13, 1812, U.S. regulars led by Lieutenant Colonel Winfield Scott and Captain John E. Wool crossed into Canada and attacked Queenston, a British settlement on the Niagara River. General Brock was killed during the fighting, but the British rallied and began to put heavy pressure on the small American force. General Stephen Van Rensselaer then ordered several thousand New York militia to cross the river and aid Scott and Wool. The militia refused to move. They had decided that their duty was to defend New York, not invade Canada. As a result, the American regulars were overwhelmed by the British, and many were forced to surrender, including Colonel Scott, who was later exchanged.

Discouraged by the behavior of his troops, General Van Rensselaer asked to be relieved of his command. He was succeeded by General Alexander Smyth, a Virginian who had been inspector general of the army. Smyth did little but make bombastic speeches to his troops, and the discouraged militia, who had little food or clothing, began leaving for home in droves.

Smyth dawdled around for several more weeks, making speeches. One speech contained these inspiring words: "Be strong! Be brave! And let the ruffian power of the British king cease on this continent!" In mid-November, 2,000 Pennsylvania militia arrived, bringing Smyth's force up to 6,000 men. He then felt that he had to make another attempt to invade Canada before winter weather put the freeze on military operations. Early in the morning of November 28, 1812, several hundred men crossed the Niagara River and seized guns on the Canadian shore. But instead of leading the rest of his troops across the river, General Smyth wasted time demanding that the British surrender Fort Erie. They refused and launched an attack that recovered the lost guns. Smyth delayed some more and finally called the whole thing off. When his happy men heard the news, they began firing their guns in all directions—many shots coming uncomfortably close to General Smyth's tent.

General Smyth went back to Virginia and was elected to Congress. Without even bothering to hold a court of inquiry, the army dropped Smyth's name from its rolls.

One more comedy of errors was played by the American forces in 1812. In mid-November, the Army of the North, which was supposed to take Montreal, moved up Lake Champlain to Plattsburgh, New York. It was commanded by Major General Henry Dearborn, who had been a dashing officer during the Revolution, but was now colorless and tired. During the night of November 19, American regulars crossed the Canadian border and clashed with Canadian troops on the La Colle River. The Canadians retreated, but in the darkness the Americans became confused and fired on one another, wounding several men. They retreated back across the border, and the New York militia once again refused to invade Canada. On November 23, Dearborn's army fell back, and all plans to invade Canada in 1812 came to a miserable end, despite the brave talk of Henry Clay and John C. Calhoun.

Much of the blame for the disasters of 1812 was placed on the state militia. But the U.S. army regulars did not do much better. Colonel Scott blamed most of the trouble on poor leadership. He said that the regulars were no match for the British when they were led by the old officers "[who] had very generally sunk into either sloth, ignorance or the habit of intemperate drinking." One disgusted American soldier said: "Our soldiers can beat their soldiers in fighting, but their generals beat ours in management."

There was, however, one officer among the New York militia who proved to have the secret of leading untrained men and making them fight.

4

BROWN TAKES COMMAND

In June of 1812, Brigadier General Jacob Brown took command of a brigade of the first detachment of New York militia mustered into the service of the United States. He was ordered to defend the eastern frontier of Lake Ontario and the southern shore of the St. Lawrence River. This defense line ran for about 200 miles from Oswego on Lake Ontario to St. Regis on the St. Lawrence at the Canadian border.

Shortly after establishing his headquarters in Brownville, Brown was busy writing letters to Governor Tompkins, letting him know the problems faced by his men. "Your Excellency will bear in mind," Brown wrote on June 26, "that this is a very new country; that the population is light and generally poor, though very respectable for so new a country, and that if any more men are called from their homes, the crops, which now promise a very abundant harvest, must perish in the ground. I mention this to your Excellency, as the country expects much more than my feeble abilities can accomplish; but no consideration of this nature shall deter me for a moment from calling out every man in the country if its defense requires it, though I must for the present hope that the force coming on will render such a measure unnecessary. I pray God that our Government will act with that decision and energy which becomes a gallant people."

Three days later, Brown wrote the governor to remind him of the duty the state owed the men who were serving the nation. "There is much uneasyness at Sackets Harbor for want of pay. These poor fellows have but a pittance for their services, and that pittance they want."

In Brown's letters is a clue to his ability to lead militia in battle. A man who worried about the crops and the pay of his volunteers knew how to win their respect and trust.

As he went about enlisting more men and collecting supplies, Brown felt that he had overstepped his authority. On July 3, he wrote Tompkins: "Upon the whole, I pray your Excellency to sanction what I have done. . . . My objective is the complete and perfect defense of this country for the present, and if I can best effect this, I shall hope to meet with the approbation of the Commander in Chief, though my conduct may be a little irregular."

This letter probably received a sympathetic response. The governor himself had run the risk of arousing the ire of the anti-war state legislature by making unauthorized military expenditures of more than $100,000.

After an inspection trip to Sackets Harbor, Brown sent an urgent letter to Tompkins on July 11: "I know and feel the effects of your Excellency's zeal for the honor and interest of the country, and I have written you so much on the subject of munitions of war that really I am almost ashamed to trouble you any more; but at the earnest solicitation of the inhabitants of this place, I must again say that without the means of arming our vessels, the lake and the river will most probably soon be at the command of the enemy, and in that case, Oswego, Ogdensburg, Sackets Harbor and Cape Vincent will be at the mercy of the enemy unless we are well supplied with ordnance for the defense of these places. And I pray your Excellency to believe me when I say that it will cost the nation twice as much to defend our frontier for twelve months as it would to conquer the Canadas in six."

Many New Yorkers opposed any plan to invade Canada. They believed that the one duty of the state militia was to defend the state. Brown was no War Hawk who wanted to seize Canadian territory, but he firmly believed that an attack on the enemy was the best defense.

By September 1812, Brown had completed the organization of his brigade and set up headquarters in Ogdensburg, New York, on the St. Lawrence River. On September 21, the commander of the regular army troops at Ogdensburg crossed the St. Lawrence to rescue prisoners that the British had taken from the area. He defeated an enemy force and then entered a village where he seized military stores and captured some prisoners. The British retaliated by bombarding Ogdensburg with guns they had stationed at Prescott, on the Canadian side of the river.

Brown, who was always busy prowling around watching the enemy, decided that the British were preparing to attack Ogdensburg. He collected 400 men and posted them along the river bank. Out of the mist came 40 boats carrying 600 British soldiers, only to be met by deadly fire from Brown's troops. Startled by the firm resistance they encountered from mere militia, the British rowed back to Prescott.

Shortly after the fight at Ogdensburg, Brown's six-month term of service in the militia expired, and he returned to his farm.

The failures of 1812 caused Congress in January 1813 to vote an increase in the number of infantry regiments in the regular army. Aiming at the handiest source of recruits, Congress invited members of the state militia to join the army for one-year terms. Secretary of War John Armstrong, who had succeeded the bumbling William Eustis, offered Brown a commission as a colonel in the regular army. Brown had watched with anger the inept leadership of Hull, Smyth, and Dearborn. He was unwilling to enter the army if required to accept a rank lower than the one he held in the militia. Brown wrote to Armstrong: "I am a full-blooded Bucks County Quaker, knowing nothing of military affairs; but I believe myself possessed of every other requisite for a soldier and an officer. I will be as good as my word. If you give me a brigade and the rank of brigadier general, you shall not be disgraced, but I will accept nothing less." Although he refused the army commission at the rank of colonel, Brown said he was ready to serve in any emergency.

5

VICTORY AT SACKETS HARBOR

In the spring of 1813, General Henry Dearborn took the American fleet and most of the troops from Sackets Harbor on Lake Ontario to attack York (now Toronto) and Fort George, at the western end of the lake. In one of his fits of absent-mindedness, the drowsy General Dearborn had left Sackets Harbor wide open to attack. When the British command at Kingston, across Lake Ontario from Sackets Harbor, heard that the defenses of the American port had been stripped, they made plans to capture it. The seizure of Sackets Harbor by the British would have given them control of Lake Ontario and a decided advantage during the fighting on the northern frontier. Commodore Isaac Chauncey, American naval commander on Lake Ontario, would have been cut off from his base of operations on the lake.

Colonel Electus Backus, an excellent officer, had been put in command of Sackets Harbor, but he had very little with which to defend it. His force consisted of the 1st and 2nd Dragoon regiments, numbering about 250 men, 50 or 60 artillerymen, and about 100 infantry, many of them ill.

General Brown, who was at his farm in Brownville a few miles away from Sackets Harbor, had been urged by General Dearborn to take command of the area. Though not wishing to interfere with his good friend Colonel Backus, Brown agreed to assume command and call out his militia in case of an attack.

On the evening of May 27, a schooner that had been scouting near Kingston came into Sackets Harbor with news that a strong British squadron, commanded by Commodore Sir James L. Yeo, had put to sea. Colonel Backus immediately sent a rider to notify General Brown. Upon hearing the news, Brown mounted his horse and rode swiftly to Sackets Harbor, eight miles away. Signal guns were fired and bells were rung in neighboring villages to summon the militia. The next day armed and unarmed men began arriving and were sent to Horse Island, where Colonel John Mills and 250 Albany volunteers were stationed. The island commanded the entrance to the harbor, and it was here that Brown believed the enemy would attempt to land. It was separated from the mainland by a shallow strait that was sometimes almost dry. On the mainland shore was a ridge of gravel about five feet high that formed a natural defensive breastwork.

Near noon on May 28, the British squadron of seven warships and two gunboats appeared off Sackets Harbor. The invasion force of more than 1,000 men consisted of several veteran British units, two regiments of Canadian militia, and a detachment of the Royal Artillery with two 6-pound cannon. There was also a large number of Indians accompanying the expedition in canoes. The whole force was commanded by Sir George Prevost, governor general of Canada. He was with Commodore Yeo on the warship *Wolfe*.

The winds became so light and uncertain that the British squadron had to anchor about six miles from Sackets Harbor. It then began to embark troops in landing boats. Suddenly signal flags fluttered on the *Wolfe,* ordering the troops to return to the squadron, which then began to turn back toward Kingston. Sir George Prevost had been alarmed by the approach of 19 American gunboats filled with troops from Oswego. The Indians shamed Sir George by darting toward the American gunboats. So he ordered several boats loaded with troops to join the Indian canoes. Twelve of the American boats carrying 70 men were captured, but seven boats with 100 men reached Sackets Harbor. There was no more action that day.

Under the cover of night, Brown withdrew Colonel Mills's force from Horse Island and placed it behind the gravel-bank breastwork on the mainland. The rest of the militia was posted on the edge of the woods a little farther back. The dragoons commanded by Colonel Backus were stationed behind the militia. The men from Oswego were posted on the left of Backus, and the artillerymen were stationed in Fort Tompkins, which had one gun, a 32-pounder.

Brown walked calmly among the militia and said: "Hide yourselves as much as possible, and do not fire until you can see the buttons of the enemy. If you are forced to retire by superior numbers, throw yourselves into the woods, rally, and assail the foe in the flank. If you cannot then stop him, retire on the left and rear of Colonel Backus and wait for further orders. Only be cool and resolute and the day is our own."

Brown's plan was to have the militia take the first assault, inflicting some damage. Then the British would have to face the fresh regulars in the second line. Brown's plan was similar to that of General Daniel Morgan at the Battle of Cowpens during the Revolutionary War. Morgan's militia had fired several volleys and then retreated around behind the regular American regiments. At the height of the battle, Morgan led the militia in an attack that helped to rout the British force.

At dawn on May 29, 33 boats loaded with redcoats

headed for Horse Island. They landed there under the protection of two gunboats commanded by Captain William Mulcaster of the Royal Navy. The boats were hammered by the big gun in Fort Tompkins and also peppered by shots from the militia. Captain Mulcaster's gunboats returned the fire, and Colonel Mills was killed.

Part of the British landing force formed up quickly on the island and pressed across the strait to the mainland. The militia began to stir uneasily as they saw the red coats and glittering bayonets of the British. They forgot Brown's instructions to be "cool and resolute." They fired one volley and began to scatter. They were led by a militia officer who had studied the approaching British and said, "I fear we shall be compelled to retreat." He took a closer look and said, "I know we shall, and as I am a little lame, I'll start now." He started running, and the rest of the men were not far behind. General Brown, who was on the left of the militia line, suddenly found himself alone. He galloped after the fugitives and attempted to rally them, but they were not listening.

On the extreme left of the militia line, a captain courageously held his ground and continued to fire a musket at the enemy after his men had fled. Finally, he started in pursuit of the militia and, with the aid of another officer, was able to rally about 100 men behind some fallen timber. From this cover, they kept up a steady fire at the advancing redcoats.

Meanwhile, Colonel Backus's dragoons and the Albany volunteers held their ground in spite of a heavy attack by the British. General Brown had just returned to the American line from his vain pursuit of the fleeing militia, when dense, black smoke arose in the rear. The Sackets Harbor storehouses, a captured British ship, and the new warship, *General Pike,* were on fire. Brown hurried to the rear to see if the enemy had landed behind the lines. He learned that a navy lieutenant, believing the battle lost, had put the torch to the storehouses and the warships. Brown returned with this news just as Colonel Backus fell mortally wounded.

The fight continued for an hour, and the Americans were slowly forced back by the overwhelming numbers of British regulars. But finally the Americans took refuge in some log barracks and were able to repulse two charges by the redcoats. The situation was touch and go, and Brown knew that his only hope was to rally the militia. First, he sent several dragoons to gallop among the scattered groups of militia and tell them that the British were retreating. Then Brown rode among them shouting: "Would you run just as we are winning! Come back and share in the victory!" These words of encouragement were spiced with harsher language that shamed the men. Fired up

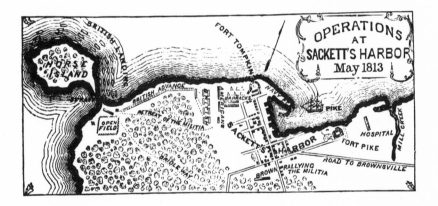

To the left on this map of the Sackets Harbor battleground, the reader can trace the route of the British as they advanced, and the path followed by the American militia as they retreated. General Brown brought his militia back through the woods and hit the British flank, forcing the enemy to make a disorderly retreat to their boats.

by Brown, 200 militia followed him in a wild bayonet charge on the British flank that threw one regiment into confusion. Fearing that his boats might be seized by Brown's rampaging militia, the cautious Prevost ordered a retreat that soon became a wild flight. The British expedition, minus 50 killed and 210 wounded, tumbled into its boats and rowed back to Yeo's ships. The Americans lost 47 killed, 84 wounded, and 36 missing—most of them militia who didn't stop running until they got home.

A large amount of supplies was lost when the storehouses burned, but the *General Pike,* which had been built of green timbers, was saved. The British ship, which had been captured at York, was saved by the quick action of an army lieutenant. Although he knew a large amount of gunpowder was on board, he boarded the ship and put out the flames. But about a half million dollars' worth of property had been lost, and the angry Brown wrote: "The Navy alone are responsible for what happened on Navy Point, and it is fortunate for them that they have reputations sufficient to sustain the shock."

At 10 A.M., Prevost sent a flag of truce and arrogantly demanded the surrender of the post he had failed to take. Brown ignored this bit of foolishness. Prevost then asked permission to send surgeons to care for the wounded that he had abandoned in his hasty retreat. Brown denied this request but assured Prevost that the wounded would be well treated, that Americans were "distinguished for humanity as well as bravery."

British critics of Prevost declared that the Sackets Harbor defeat was "in high degree disgraceful." Commodore Yeo was opposed to the retreat and reported that one officer, Major William Drummond, had protested to Prevost: "Allow me a few moments, Sir, and I will put you in possession of this place." The nervous Prevost snapped: "Obey your orders, Sir, and learn the first duty of a soldier."

Brown's excellent leadership under great difficulties was praised throughout the country, and Secretary of War Armstrong hastened to give him the commission as brigadier general in the regular army that Brown had requested earlier. The ex-schoolteacher and surveyor had proved his military abilities beyond a doubt.

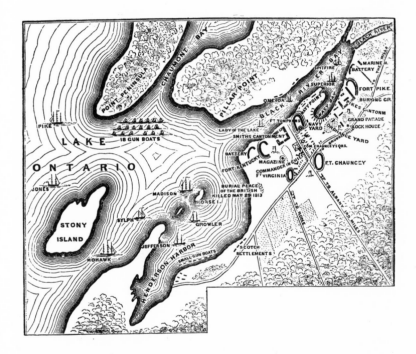

This map of Sackets Harbor in 1814 shows the extensive fortifications that Commodore Chauncey and General Brown had ordered constructed to protect this vital American naval base on Lake Ontario.

The British never again attacked Sackets Harbor. It remained the most important supply depot for the army and navy on the northern frontier. Brown's victory was one of the few bright spots in the war until Perry beat the British fleet on Lake Erie in September 1813. The next month, Harrison's army routed the British and Indians. The ground lost by Hull's surrender of Detroit had been regained.

6

LOST OPPORTUNITIES

General Dearborn's expedition against York, for which he had withdrawn most of the forces from Sackets Harbor, had started well but then frittered away its gains. On April 25, 1813, Commodore Chauncey's fleet, carrying 1,700 soldiers, left Oswego on Lake Ontario. Two days later, the ships anchored three miles west of York, then capital of Upper Canada. On April 28, a force of 1,600 men commanded by Brigadier General Zebulon M. Pike hit the beach at York and scattered the British and Canadian defenders. (Pike was an outstanding Western explorer whose name is honored by Pikes Peak, Colorado.)

After the Americans had taken York, a magazine containing 500 barrels of gunpowder exploded, showering the Americans and British with timbers and stone. Pike was mortally wounded, while 38 of his men were killed and 222 wounded. The British lost 40 men, and an unknown number were wounded. Major General Sir Roger Hale Sheaffe, the governor of Upper Canada, withdrew his troops eastward to Kingston. One of Dearborn's mistakes was to neglect to police York properly. As a result, American soldiers and local criminals looted houses and burned the parliament building. The British later retaliated by burning the President's House (later called the White House) and the Capitol when they captured Washington in 1814.

Worried by reports that Commodore Yeo had a strong naval force near York, Dearborn and Chauncey gave up the town. They sailed their troops and fleet to Four Mile Creek on Lake Ontario near Fort Niagara. Then the American commanders sat around wondering what to do next.

But two of their young officers were making plans. Colonel Winfield Scott, who had been exchanged after his capture at Queenston, was now Dearborn's adjutant general. Master Commandant Oliver Hazard Perry had been busy building ships at Presque Isle (now Erie, Pennsylvania) on Lake Erie. They persuaded their slowpoke commanders, Dearborn and Chauncey, to let them launch the first truly amphibious operation in the history of the U.S. Army and Navy.

On May 24, 1813, Perry's ships escorted Scott's assault force of 134 boats and barges. The troops landed near Fort George, the British stronghold at the Lake Ontario end of the Niagara River. After a two-hour fight, British Brigadier General John Vincent abandoned Fort George and ordered his battered troops to retreat westward along Lake Ontario to Burlington. Now, Scott saw his great opportunity to pursue and capture Vincent's whole force. But to Scott's disgust, Brigadier General Morgan Lewis, Dearborn's second in command, ordered the pursuit halted.

Scott raged around headquarters, demanding an advance before Vincent could reorganize his troops. But the sick, fluttery Dearborn did not order pursuit until June 1. The pursuing force was commanded by Brigadier General William H. Winder, a Baltimore lawyer with scant military knowledge. Four days later, Winder was reinforced by a brigade commanded by Brigadier General John Chandler, a politician, tavern-keeper, and Revolutionary War veteran. Winder and Chandler proved to be highly incompetent. Although their camp at Stoney Creek was only a few miles east of Vincent's outposts, the American commanders failed to send out strong patrols during the night. Early in the morning of June 6, British red-coats swarmed into the camp, scattered the Americans, and captured Winder and Chandler.

General Dearborn now ordered Brigadier General Lewis to take command of all American troops. Lewis was to move along a coastal road to attack the British at Burlington Heights. This route exposed Lewis's troops to shelling from Commo-dore Yeo's ships on Lake Ontario. The Americans also were harassed by roving bands of Indians. To make matters worse, Lewis was confused by orders from Dearborn that seemed to tell him to advance and retreat at the same time. And Com-modore Chauncey's fleet made no effort to keep Yeo's ships from throwing shells into Lewis's troops. By now thoroughly confused and frightened, Lewis ordered a retreat that did not end until his force was back at Fort George.

The defeat at Stoney Creek and Lewis's retreat were too much for the ailing Dearborn. He took to his bed and turned over his command to Lewis. Since Lewis had gone to Sackets Harbor for a rest, Brigadier General John Boyd became the commander at Fort George. Boyd was described by the out-spoken Colonel Scott as a "vacillating . . . imbecile beyond all endurance." Unfortunately, Boyd thought he ought to do something to wipe out the memory of recent army blunders. Hearing that General Vincent had established an outpost only 16 miles away from Fort George, Boyd ordered Lieutenant Colonel Charles G. Boerstler to take 500 army regulars and attack the British. Moving carelessly through the woods, Boer-stler's troops were ambushed by a small force of British and

Indians who forced them to surrender. Most of the American wounded were killed by the Indians. The captured Americans were taken to York.

Dearborn lamely called Boerstler's defeat "an unfortunate and unaccountable event." Too many such events convinced President Madison and Secretary of War Armstrong that Dearborn had to go. He was relieved of his command early in July 1813. While Dearborn's replacement, Major General James Wilkinson, was on his way north to take command, Boyd remained in charge.

Still anxious to win some glory for the army, Boyd proposed an attack on the British supply depot at Burlington Heights on Lake Ontario. Fortunately, Boyd picked the energetic Colonel Scott to lead the raid. Commodore Chauncey's fleet carried Scott's force to Burlington Heights on July 29, but found the place bristling with guns. Determined not to go home empty-handed, Scott proposed an attack on York, which had been stripped of guns and troops to defend Burlington Heights. Chauncey agreed and carried Scott's troops the 40 miles up the lake and they landed unopposed at York. The prisoners from Boerstler's ill-fated command were rescued, and military supplies that could not be carried away were destroyed. No gains in territory had been made, but the army and navy had shown an ability to work together. Even more important, Colonel Scott had exhibited the energy and leadership that were later to be put to good use by Brigadier General Brown.

Action on the northern frontier now switched from land to water. On August 7, 1813, the fleets of Commodore Chauncey and Commodore Yeo finally faced each other in battle formation on Lake Ontario. Chauncey, whose ships had more long-range guns than Yeo's, wanted to fight at a distance. Yeo, who had more heavy, short-range guns, wanted to get at close quarters. Therefore, both commanders maneuvered cautiously throughout August 7, and not a gun was fired. That night, a violent storm struck, and the two largest American schooners sank with the loss of most of their crews. At daybreak the lake had calmed, and the fleets went back to their game of "I dare you."

All through the 8th, 9th, and 10th of August, the British and American ships paraded past each other, out of range. At the end of each day, Yeo and Chauncey wrote reports accusing the other of running away from a fight. On the night of August 10, the wind, which had been light, began to shift and stiffen. The fleets drew near and began to exchange shots. At this critical moment, two American schooners became separated from the fleet and were captured. Having lost four ships, and being short of supplies, Chauncey retreated to Sackets Harbor.

Reinforced by a new schooner late in August, Chauncey again took his fleet out on Lake Ontario. In September came the startling news of Perry's victory on Lake Erie. For the first time in history, an entire British fleet had been forced to surrender. Apparently fired up by this news, Chauncey went looking for Yeo and found him on September 28. The American gunnery proved to be much more accurate than that of the British, and Yeo's ships took a pounding. Sorely hurt, the British began a scrambling retreat. Chauncey had an opportunity to wreck the enemy fleet, but he was too cautious. He stalled around to wait for his slower ships, and let the British escape into Burlington Bay. Because of Chauncey's slow-footedness in chasing Yeo, this engagement is known in history not as a battle but as "the Burlington Races."

Chauncey could still have beaten Yeo's fleet. Burlington Bay was open water and several of the strongest British ships were crippled. But Chauncey pulled his ships away from Burlington Bay and began making excuses for not fighting: his flagship, *General Pike,* had lost a gun; the wind was rising and might drive his ships on the shore. He was still thinking up excuses the next day when a gale did begin. When it had blown itself out, Yeo had slipped past Chauncey's fleet and had sailed back to Kingston.

On the water, as on land, the Lake Ontario campaign had ended in a mess. Commodore Chauncey's fumbling performance is detailed here because he later figures in Brown's campaign on the Niagara frontier. There, again, Chauncey's caution and ability to think up excuses for not acting were to prove most trying to Brown. The example of army-navy teamwork with Winfield Scott at Fort George and York was forgotten by Chauncey.

7

WILKINSON AND DISASTER

Early in 1813, Secretary of War Armstrong decided that the command of the army was "a burden too heavy for General Dearborn to carry." Armstrong considered two remedies. One was to fire Dearborn immediately; the other was to add officers to his staff who would "secure to the Army better instruction, and to himself the chance of wiser councils." The second remedy was chosen. Major General James Wilkinson, commanding the Gulf of Mexico region, and Major General Wade Hampton, stationed at Norfolk, Virginia, were ordered to the northern frontier to aid Dearborn.

Wilkinson and Armstrong had been members of General Horatio Gates's staff during the Revolutionary War campaign that resulted in the capture of Burgoyne's army at Saratoga in 1777. General Hampton was an aristocratic Southern plantation owner who served with the guerrilla forces of "Swamp Fox" Francis Marion in South Carolina during the Revolution. Unfortunately, Wilkinson and Hampton were bitter enemies and so jealous of each other that they would not cooperate. The idea that these two men could provide Dearborn with "wiser councils" was too silly to consider seriously—except by Armstrong.

Wilkinson was not eager to go north where the climate might harm his health, which had not been good for several years. Fat, ruddy-faced, and overly fond of food and drink, Wilkinson strutted around in gaudy uniforms. He was a shrewd man who had the principles of a burglar. In sending orders to Wilkinson, Armstrong enclosed a private letter that breathed goodwill: "Why should you remain in your land of cypress," wrote Armstrong, "when patriotism and ambition equally invite you to one where grows the laurel . . .? If our cards be well-played, we may renew the scenes of Saratoga." Wilkinson couldn't have known much about patriotism, but ambition prompted him to obey Armstrong's orders.

Throughout his career, Wilkinson had been a devious, scheming, and incompetent officer and a troublemaker. While serving as military commander in Louisiana, he had been a paid agent of the Spanish government. He was also involved in Aaron Burr's wild scheme to carve out an empire in the Southwest, but had turned against Burr when he thought it would be to his advantage. Wilkinson gave testimony to the grand jury that indicted Burr for treason, and the jury wound up nearly indicting Wilkinson too. The American statesman John Randolph of Roanoke summed him up: "Wilkinson is the only man I ever saw who was from the bark to the core a villain." Wilkinson had been court-martialed twice for his many misdeeds, but had not been convicted.

Wilkinson took his time about traveling north. When he reached Washington on July 31, Armstrong had finally fired Dearborn. Wilkinson was formally given command of the Army of the North. Though weary from travel and sickness, Wilkinson did get around to discussing a plan of campaign. Armstrong proposed a concentration of forces at Sackets Harbor and an attack on Kingston. His alternate plan called for a two-pronged attack down the St. Lawrence. One force from Sackets Harbor and another moving from Plattsburgh would combine at Montreal to block the river and cut British communications on the St. Lawrence.

Nothing was settled while Wilkinson was in Washington, but as he traveled north toward Sackets Harbor, he wrote a letter that brushed aside Armstrong's proposals. He came up with a plan that had American forces striking out in all directions. "Will it not be better," Wilkinson wrote on August 6, "to strengthen our force already at Fort George, cut up the British in that quarter, destroy Indian establishments, and should General Harrison fail in his object [to retake Detroit] march a detachment and capture Malden? After which, closing our operations on the peninsula [Niagara] . . . descend like lightning with our whole force on Kingston, and, having reduced that place . . . go down the St. Lawrence and form a junction with Hampton's column [from Plattsburgh], if the lateness of the season should permit."

It was typical of the scheming Wilkinson to try to downgrade General Harrison, whose military reputation was much better than his. It was also typical of Wilkinson to give no thought to the problem of getting the men and supplies needed for his far-flung campaign.

Armstrong, who liked to run things to suit himself, was quick to get impatient when his opinions were disputed. He began to dislike his old companion in arms whom he had invited north to win laurels. In his reply to Wilkinson, Armstrong flatly rejected a campaign on the Niagara peninsula or farther west to Fort Malden. An attack on Malden, he said, would merely "wound the tail of the lion." Instead of launching an immediate attack on Kingston, Armstrong suggested that Wilkinson might go down the St. Lawrence, join the column from Plattsburgh, take Montreal, and then return and capture Kingston.

During his trip to Sackets Harbor, Wilkinson sent his first orders as commander in chief of the Army of the North to Wade Hampton at Plattsburgh. When he had ordered Hampton to Plattsburgh, Armstrong had implied that this command was independent of Wilkinson's, though it was definitely in Wilkinson's military district. So Wilkinson's sending of orders to Hampton aroused the ire of the old aristocrat. He owned huge plantations and thousands of slaves in South Carolina and Louisiana and seemed to feel that this qualified him to lead men into battle. Hampton wrote Armstrong that he would resign if he had to take orders from Wilkinson. Armstrong soothed Hampton by arranging to have Wilkinson's orders to him sent through the War Department. In September, Armstrong moved his office as secretary of war to Sackets Harbor, presumably to handle the messages of his warring commanders. But Armstrong's main reason for moving north was to direct the coming campaign free from any supervision by President Madison. Armstrong enjoyed power and fancied himself a military expert. Above all, he was a busybody and a faultfinder who encouraged others to find fault. From start to finish, this campaign was an example of what not to do.

Before Armstrong got into the middle of things at Sackets Harbor, Wilkinson had written him a sassy letter: "I trust you will not interfere with my arrangements, or give orders within the district of my command . . . because it would impair my authority and distract the public service. Two heads on the same shoulders make a monster."

An observer of the Armstrong-Wilkinson-Hampton tangle commented: "Unhappily for the country, that deplorable campaign was a monster with three heads, biting and barking at each other with a madness which destroyed them all and disgusted the country."

Wilkinson's Army of the North was supposed to contain more than 12,000 men. Four thousand were in the right wing, under Hampton at Plattsburgh. The center wing was at Sackets Harbor. The left wing was at Fort George, the occupied British post on the Canadian side of the Niagara River. Sickness had, however, cut the effective force down to around 9,000. The rations consisted of salt pork or salt beef, dried peas, bread, and whiskey. Much of the flour was spoiled, and the bakers mixed their dough with inshore water that was polluted by the latrines. Many men were ill with dysentery.

In August 1813, of the 3,483 men at Sackets Harbor, only 2,042 were fit for duty. Lack of clothing also contributed to the ill health of the troops. No waterproof garments had been issued. Shoes were made of leather described "as porous as sponge." A soldier was lucky to have a greatcoat for protection against snow and rain. More often, the men had to wrap themselves in a blanket or a piece of oilcloth torn from a meat keg. Their uniforms were more suited for dress parade and warm weather than for winter campaigns along the frigid St. Lawrence and the Great Lakes.

Only one regular army regiment, the 5th, had been organized for more than a year and had been properly trained. The men in the other army regiments were called regulars, but they didn't deserve the name. Most of their officers were as green and untrained as their men. Colonel Scott said the officers were generally "coarse, ignorant men," with a scattering of "educated swaggerers, decayed gentlemen and others unfit for anything else."

The high command of the army was little better than the men in the ranks. Wilkinson, who was incompetent, was surrounded by incompetents. His second in command, Brigadier General Morgan Lewis, was feeble and often ill. Brigadier General John Boyd had proved his lack of ability at Fort George. Brigadier General Robert Swartwout tried to command an infantry brigade and also serve as quartermaster general. This task would have taxed the abilities of a genius, which Swartwout definitely wasn't. Brigadier General Moses Porter, the chief of artillery, was fairly bright but too old to stand a hard campaign. These men could neither train nor inspire troops, and Secretary of War Armstrong's meddling and faultfinding merely added to the confusion and bungling.

There were a few younger officers who were yet to prove their full worth: Brigadier General Brown, Colonel Scott, Colonel Alexander Macomb, and Colonel John D. Walbach. Wilkinson could not have been too happy to have Scott, an old enemy, around. Their dislike for each other dated from 1809. At that time, Wilkinson, commanding troops in New Orleans, was directed to move them upriver to a higher, healthier location. Instead, he moved them downriver to a swampy, mosquito-infested area that was half-flooded during the summer. In addition, Wilkinson was a friend of the contractor who supplied the army with sour bread crawling with worms, and spoiled pork and beef. In less than a year, 1,000 men died and 40 officers resigned or died.

Young Captain Scott remained healthy and full of fight. He ignored discipline and called Wilkinson a traitor, liar, and scoundrel. For this Scott was court-martialed in 1810, convicted, and sentenced to "be suspended from all rank . . . for the space of 12 months." It was a mild sentence (Scott could have been dismissed from the army) and, surprisingly, the court even recommended that Scott's suspension be cut to three months. Not so surprisingly, the recommendation was not approved by the department commander—Wilkinson. So Scott returned to his home town of Petersburg, Virginia, and spent a year studying military history and tactics, which proved valuable to the army and General Brown in 1814.

Ignoring his enemy Scott, Wilkinson worked up a violent dislike of General Brown because he had refused to serve under the incompetent General Boyd. Wilkinson wrote that Brown "knows not enough of military duty to post the guards in a camp." He accused Brown of coddling his men and playing politics to win advancement in the army. The facts were that Brown's brigade had fewer men sick than any other in the army. He was the only brigade commander who made his men build snug huts with fireplaces, proper drainage, and latrines. The men worshiped Brown, and Wilkinson could not stand that.

On the other hand, Colonel Scott, who was harsh in his judgment of many officers, wrote that Brown "was not a technical soldier, that is, knew little of organization, tactics, police, etc., but was of great value because of his zeal and vigor." Although Brown, the former militia officer, had been promoted over Scott, they got along well together. They were more interested in fighting the enemy than each other, which couldn't be said of Wilkinson, Hampton, and many other officers.

On August 28, before Armstrong's arrival, Wilkinson called a council of his officers at Sackets Harbor. It was attended by Lewis, Brown, Swartwout, and Commodore Chauncey. The council decided to concentrate all troops at Sackets Harbor, except for those at Plattsburgh, and prepare to strike "a deadly blow somewhere"—still not a very clear plan of action. Wilkinson then hurried to Fort George to inspect the troops there. He arrived at Fort George on September 4, suffering from chills and fever brought on by six days of traveling across Lake Ontario in an open boat in a cold rain. From this time on, until he was relieved of his command, Wilkinson was plagued by ill health.

In those days, for such ailments as fever and "camp ills," opium was prescribed, and Wilkinson apparently used it regularly. He was reported to have been "high" on laudanum (an opium preparation) while traveling down the St. Lawrence to attack Montreal the following November. Wilkinson's use of this drug would help to explain his unstable behavior, his faulty judgment, and his impossible campaign proposals. Easily alarmed by reports of enemy activity, he made decisions too quickly and was too slow to correct his mistakes. His errors might have been disregarded if he had been an inspiring leader, but he wasn't.

While at Fort George, Wilkinson received orders from Armstrong in Sackets Harbor to strengthen that post and leave a strong force of regulars and New York militia there. Colonel Scott was put in command at Fort George, which annoyed him as he felt he would have little chance to fight.

When Wilkinson returned to Sackets Harbor, he had several conferences with his officers and Secretary of War Armstrong. Finally, a decision was reached to ignore Kingston and move down the St. Lawrence against Montreal. Meanwhile, General Hampton's army was to advance from Plattsburgh along the Chateaugay River toward the St. Lawrence.

During August and September, scores of armed boats and transports for troops had been built at Sackets Harbor. Commodore Chauncey's fleet took time off from playing tag with Yeo's ships to carry supplies to Wilkinson's army. Everything was reported in readiness on October 4. But final orders were not issued by Wilkinson until the 12th. His elaborate plans called for each unit to carry a flag on its boats so the commanding general could quickly locate it. Four more days were wasted while the weather showed signs of changing. Old-timers sniffed the breeze and warned that the time was ripe for a sudden violent storm. But their advice was ignored.

Recklessly disregarding the risks involved, Wilkinson ordered 8,000 troops embarked on the night of October 17. They were jammed in scows, barges, and lake sailboats, with guns, ammunition, hospital stores, baggage, and two months' provisions. This flotilla was expected to pick its way among islands and past points of land where the depth of the water was not known. Experienced pilots were scarce, and the success of the expedition seemed to have been trusted to luck. Luck did not last long. After midnight the night they embarked, the wind rose and before morning a savage gale, loaded with rain and sleet, lashed Lake Ontario. The flotilla was scattered in all directions. A gloomy dawn showed the shores of islands and the mainland strewn with the wreckage of boats and supplies. Fifteen large boats were wrecked and dozens more were too heavily damaged to be safe. The storm lasted 36 hours, and most of the troops did not reach their reunion point on Grenadier Island (where Lake Ontario flows into the St. Lawrence) until October 20.

The worried General Wilkinson busied himself with traveling between Sackets Harbor and Grenadier Island, trying to put his expedition back together. A report on October 22 showed that a large number of troops were still packed in vessels that had been wrecked or driven ashore. The weather still refused to cooperate, and Wilkinson finally wrote to Armstrong on October 24: "The extent of the injury to our craft, clothing, arms and provisions greatly exceeds our apprehensions, and has subjected us to the necessity of furnishing clothing, and of making repairs and equipments to the flotilla generally. In fact, all our hopes have been nearly blasted; but, thanks to the same Providence that placed us in jeopardy, we are surmounting our difficulties, and, God willing, I shall pass Prescott [opposite Ogdensburg on the St. Lawrence] on the night of the 1st or 2nd [of November]."

Storm after storm swept Lake Ontario and the St. Lawrence. Wilkinson's troops on Grenadier Island soon were slogging through snow 10 inches deep. Food was scarce, and the men crouched in brush shelters and tents and tried to keep warm over smoky fires of green wood. With the always savage Canadian winter approaching, Wilkinson had to act immediately. Despite the bad weather, General Brown's brigade was ordered to push down the St. Lawrence as an advance guard on October 29. He reached French Creek and made camp in a thick woods near the present village of Clayton, New York.

Meanwhile, General Hampton was moving down the Chateaugay River toward the St. Lawrence. On October 25, near the town of Spear's (now Howick, Quebec), the American advance was opposed by 1,000 troops, mostly Canadian militia, commanded by the vigilant and vigorous Colonel Charles M. De Salaberry. That night, General Hampton directed Colonel Robert Purdy to take about 2,000 men, cross the Chateaugay, and attack the enemy from the rear in the morning. The sound of Purdy's guns was to be the signal for the rest of Hampton's army to attack. Purdy's movement was hampered by darkness and the ignorance of the guides assigned to him. After crossing the river, the guides got lost in a hemlock swamp and could find neither the river nor the point from where they started. Purdy's troops wandered around all night. Units bumped into each other in the darkness and scuffled nervously. In the morning, Purdy finally got his men out of the swamp and allowed them to rest a half mile from the river. In a later report to Wilkinson, the angry Purdy wrote: "Incredible as it may appear, General Hampton intrusted nearly one half of his army, and those his best troops, to the guidance of men, each of whom repeatedly assured him that they were not acquainted with the country, and were not competent to direct such an expedition."

Hours passed, and Hampton waited impatiently for the sound of Purdy's guns. Finally, at two o'clock in the afternoon, Hampton ordered Brigadier General George Izard to attack the enemy's entrenchments. The courageous Colonel De Salaberry opposed him with 300 Canadians and a few Abenake Indians but was driven back by Izard's overwhelming numbers.

Firing now was heard across the Chateaugay River. Purdy, who had failed to post guards, had been surprised by a small force of Canadian militia. The Americans panicked and fled to the river. Several officers and men swam across and told Hampton that a large enemy force was on the other side. That "large" force had actually fled after firing on Purdy's troops. Both sides had run away from each other. Some of Purdy's troops, who plunged back into the hemlock swamp, mistook each other for enemies and had a spirited little fight. This blunder cost the life of one man.

Colonel De Salaberry, a thinking as well as a fighting man, decided to trick the already jumpy Hampton. He posted buglers far out on the ends of his line. Then some concealed militia fired on the Americans while the buglers sounded the charge. The alarmed Hampton thought he was being attacked on both flanks as well as the front. He ordered a retreat to Four Corners (now Chateaugay), New York, where his campaign ended in disgrace.

Never had so many Americans been beaten by so few enemies on foreign soil. Major John E. Wool of the 29th Infantry Regiment said disgustedly, "No officer who had any regard for his reputation would voluntarily acknowledge himself as having been engaged in" the battle at Chateaugay.

The British reaction to Wilkinson's campaign down the St. Lawrence had been delayed by bad news from the West. On October 5 General William Henry Harrison had smashed the British and Indians on the Thames River and appeared ready to invade Upper Canada. To meet this threat, General Vincent was ordered to withdraw his troops from the Fort George area and concentrate them at Burlington Heights. Colonel Scott's orders required him to leave Fort George with his regulars and join Wilkinson if the British withdrew from the area. So when Vincent moved his troops west, the impatient Scott lost no time in turning command of Fort George over to General George McClure of the New York militia. Scott joined the Wilkinson expedition at Ogdensburg, New York, on the St. Lawrence.

Secretary of War Armstrong, who disliked Harrison, saw to it that Harrison gave the British no trouble. He ordered Harrison to send his militia home and turn one of his brigades over to Wilkinson. Finally, Armstrong sent Harrison to command the Cincinnati area, far from the fighting. Harrison soon resigned in disgust.

Sir George Prevost dispatched troops to oppose Hampton, and ordered naval and land forces at Kingston to do something about Wilkinson. Commodore Chauncey's fleet attempted a blockade of Kingston in order to keep the British from sending forces down the St. Lawrence to nip at Wilkinson's flotilla. But British marine scouts soon were prowling around in the St. Lawrence.

On November 1, the British scouts discovered Brown's brigade at French Creek, which was only about 20 miles from Kingston. That same day, two brigs, two schooners, and eight gunboats loaded with British troops attacked the Americans under Brown. But, unlike other American officers, Brown was ready for trouble. He had planted a battery of three guns on the western shore of French Creek. These guns battered the British flotilla and forced it to retreat. At dawn the next morning, the stubborn British returned, but were again driven off with heavy losses. Brown lost only two men killed and four wounded.

On November 3, Wilkinson reached French Creek with the rest of the expedition. On the 5th, a clear, crisp morning, the American flotilla, consisting of around 300 boats, moved on down the river. The British soon had a heavily armed galley and several gunboats filled with troops nagging at the rear of the American flotilla. To avoid heavy damage from the guns posted at Prescott, opposite Ogdensburg, Wilkinson halted three miles above those towns. There, he landed his ammunition and all his troops, except for enough men to handle the boats. The troops were to march to Red Mills, four

Major General Jacob Brown.

Brigadier General Winfield Scott.   President John Quincy Adams.

Secretary of War John Armstrong.

As the tide of battle at Lundy's Lane turned in favor of the Americans, General Brown was shot through the hip and also hit in the side by a shell fragment.

During the Battle of Chippewa, General Winfield Scott saw that the British lines were disorganized and ordered McNeil's regiment to charge, splitting the enemy lines and forcing the British to withdraw.

Jackson's militia cut down British regulars in the Battle of New Orleans.

General Andrew Jackson, famous for the victory of his militia at New Orleans, had to admit afterward that he had not attempted to fight the British regulars in open country because his men were largely untrained. Jacob Brown, on the other hand, had broken the enemy with his militia by a direct attack at Fort Erie.

miles below Ogdensburg on the American side of the river. The boats under General Brown were to run past the guns of Prescott that night.

At this time, Wilkinson was visited by Hampton's adjutant general. Wilkinson sent him back to Hampton with an order to push on to the St. Lawrence and meet him at St. Regis on the Canadian border. This order from his old enemy did nothing but raise Hampton's blood pressure. He already had decided to call off his campaign. Hampton's decision was influenced by news that Armstrong had ordered winter quarters for 10,000 men to be built far south of Montreal. It appeared that Armstrong had lost faith in Wilkinson and Hampton. Hampton said the news "sank my hopes and raised serious doubts of receiving that . . . support which had been anticipated."

The American flotilla moved downriver at eight o'clock in the evening of November 5 under cover of a heavy fog. General Brown led the way in a small boat. When Brown's boat was opposite Prescott, the fog suddenly lifted and the moon shone brightly. Cannon boomed and shots splashed all around Brown's boat. He calmly signaled for the flotilla to halt until the moon went down. Later, the flotilla moved on. The guns of Prescott continued to boom, but only two boats failed to make the passage. These two boats ran aground near Ogdensburg, but were floated free and later joined the others at Red Mills. Wilkinson then got word that the Canadian shore downriver was lined with infantry and artillery posts to oppose the passage of the flotilla. To meet this threat, on November 7 he sent Colonel Alexander Macomb to land with 1,200 men on the Canadian shore.

The flotilla arrived at a point about 18 miles below Ogdensburg on November 8. There, Wilkinson called a council of officers consisting of Generals Lewis, Boyd, Brown, Porter, Swartwout, and Leonard Covington. They heard a gloomy report from Colonel Joseph G. Swift (who was the first graduate of West Point) on the strength of enemy forces both behind and ahead of the expedition. Wilkinson's officers decided to push on with all possible speed, but they were not very confident of taking Montreal. Their feelings were well expressed by Covington and Porter: "We proceed from this place under great danger . . . but . . . we know of no other alternative."

To put more pressure on the enemy, General Brown was sent across the river with his brigade to aid Colonel Macomb's troops. Colonel Scott now commanded a unit in Brown's brigade. While Brown's men were going into action downriver, Wilkinson received disturbing news from upriver. British reinforcements had been sent from Kingston to Prescott under the command of Colonel Joseph W. Morrison. They had come in two schooners and several gunboats commanded by Captain Mulcaster, which had slipped through Commodore Chauncey's careless blockade of Kingston. On November 9, this force was close behind Wilkinson. Accordingly, Brigadier General Boyd's brigade was ordered to act as a rear guard and attack the pursuing enemy if necessary.

Wilkinson was in a tight corner. British vessels were pursuing the American flotilla and land forces were lurking in the rear, ready to team up with the British gunboats in an attack on the Americans. Canadian militia continually nipped at the heels of Boyd's brigade in the rear. Other forces delayed Brown and Macomb in their expedition across the river by felling trees across roads and burning bridges.

On the morning of November 10, the flotilla neared the "Longue Sault," a dangerous eight-mile stretch of rapids in the St. Lawrence. Brown reported that the British had built a strong blockhouse at the foot of the rapids. The flotilla halted while Brown pushed ahead to capture the blockhouse. At noon, a roar of cannon indicated that Brown was at work. At that moment, British gunboats began peppering the rear of the American flotilla. This attack was not beaten off until evening, so Wilkinson decided to halt at Chrysler's Field on the Canadian side of the river. General Boyd, commanding the rear guard, camped nearby.

At ten o'clock on the stormy morning of November 11, Wilkinson, still camped at Chrysler's Field, received a message from Brown. He said the enemy had been cleared from the blockhouse at Longue Sault and urged Wilkinson to move quickly with supplies. In his reply, the ailing Wilkinson told Brown of the attacks on the rear of the flotilla and said he feared enemy gunboats might pass him and strengthen the British forces downriver. Feeling very sorry for himself, Wilkinson said he was writing "from my bed," and went on to say: "It is now that I feel the heavy hand of disease—enfeebled and confined to my bed while the safety of the army intrusted to my command, the honor of our armies, and the greatest interests of our country are at hazard." Wilkinson wrote a speech when he should have been giving orders to his troops.

The ailing commander at last roused himself and ordered the flotilla to proceed. Moments later he was informed that British infantry was advancing, and that their gunboats were preparing to attack. Wilkinson ordered the flotilla to re-anchor, and told General Boyd to oppose the British force under Colonel Morrison. Boyd had three times as many men as Morrison, but he sent his brigades into action one at a time and they were badly mauled by the British.

In another action with the British, General Covington was killed and his troops fell back in disorder. Other brigades faltered, and the British launched an attack that threatened to capture the American cannon. A wild cavalry charge led by Colonel Walbach saved the guns.

The battle at Chrysler's Field had been going on for almost five hours in a storm of snow and sleet when the whole American line began to retreat. The retreat was becoming a

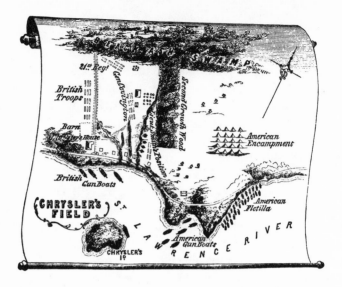

The mismanagement of his superior force by General Boyd resulted in a costly defeat for the Americans during the advance down the St. Lawrence toward Montreal.

rout until Lieutenant Colonel Timothy Upham of the 21st Regiment led 600 fresh men into action. Upham's troops checked the British advance. But the rest of Boyd's force retreated to the boats of the flotilla. The Americans lost 102 killed and 237 wounded. The British lost 22 killed, 150 wounded, and 15 missing.

The morning after the Battle of Chrysler's Field, the flotilla passed safely down the rapids. Three miles above Cornwall, across the river from St. Regis, the expedition joined the forces commanded by General Brown. Wilkinson now expected to hear of Hampton's arrival at St. Regis, but he was disappointed. The day before, Brown had sent a message to Hampton telling him of the battle at Chrysler's Field and saying: "My own opinion is you can not be with us too soon."

While Wilkinson was stewing over Hampton's absence, Hampton's inspector general arrived with a message dated November 11. In it, Hampton said he was at Four Corners and had no intention of joining Wilkinson. The enraged Wilkinson shouted that he would "arrest Hampton and direct General Izard to bring forward the division." But he was too weakened in body and mind to carry out this threat, so he contented himself with uttering a few curses.

That day, November 12, a council of Wilkinson's officers decided that "the conduct of Major General Hampton, in refusing to join his division [with] the troops descending the St. Lawrence, rendered it expedient to remove the army to French Mills on the Salmon River." Colonel Swift reported that the younger members of the council believed "that with Brown as leader" the army could go on to Montreal. But the majority of the officers opposed such a move. On the following day, November 13, when a large British force was reported nearby, the troops were hastily embarked on boats under General Brown's command. They sailed for the Salmon River and went into winter quarters near French Mills (now Fort Covington, New York).

Long before the expedition had reached its dreary end, Secretary of War Armstrong had gone back to Washington. When he saw that Wilkinson and Hampton had botched things up beyond repair, Armstrong skipped out to escape blame for the failure.

Wilkinson did not go to French Mills. Pleading ill health, he headed down the Salmon River to Malone, New York, after transferring command of the army to General Lewis. Lewis and Boyd both obtained leaves of absence, and command of the army went to General Brown. Hampton, meanwhile, had moved his troops back to Plattsburgh. Wilkinson directed Hampton to join Brown at French Mills. But this, like other orders from Wilkinson, was ignored by Hampton. Leaving General Izard in command at Plattsburgh, Hampton retired to his plantation in Louisiana, much to the relief of the army.

On November 24, General Brown wrote to Armstrong from French Mills: "You have learned that the grand army of the United States, after marching and countermarching most ingloriously, arrived at this place on the 13th. I must now express to you my indignation and sorrow." Then Brown got a dig in at Armstrong: "I did not expect you would have left us." In the same letter, he added: "Colonel Scott will hand you this, and can give you all the information you wish relative to our movements since he joined us, and the present situation of our army. The public interest would be promoted by the advancement of such men as Scott."

Brown had comfortable quarters in a house on the bank of the Salmon River, but he spent little time there. He was out in the snow and the biting wind day after day, directing the building of snug huts for his troops. Most of the men had lost their blankets and extra clothing in the storms on Lake Ontario or in the Battle of Chrysler's Field. The country around French Mills was a wilderness, and provisions were scarce. But the determined Brown kept ordering parties out daily to scour the countryside for food and firewood. Most of the medicines and hospital stores had been lost through careless management, and replacements could be obtained only in Albany, 250 miles away. The death rate among the sick soared, and disease disabled nearly one-half of the army before the men were housed in huts. Brown grimly wrote that five men died of disease for each one who fell in battle because of a policy that assumed that the soldier "could bear all the vicissitudes of climate and weather without requiring either quarters or covering."

Brown's unending fight to get better food, clothing, and housing for his men annoyed Wilkinson, who remained in his comfortable quarters at Malone. During the St. Lawrence expedition, Wilkinson had been quick to call on Brown when there was heavy fighting to be done. Now, he called Brown "a dirty dog." Sticking in Wilkinson's warped mind was the fact that many officers thought the army could have taken Montreal if Brown had been in command.

When he wasn't sniping at Brown, Wilkinson was concocting wild plans to rescue his damaged reputation. He wrote of striking the British a blow that would "reach the bone," and insisted that action was needed to keep the troops from "eating the bread of idleness." During January 1814, Wilkinson presented two plans for an invasion of Canada. Both were laid aside when it became clear, even to Wilkinson, that neither the food, winter clothing, ammunition, nor troops were available. As previously mentioned, it is quite possible that he was high on laudanum when he made these plans.

Because of British threats to attack the camp at French Mills, the War Department ordered Wilkinson to abandon it. Wilkinson sent orders to Brown, and, early in February 1814, the boats were burned and the hospital at Malone abandoned. Brown, who had been promoted to major general in the regular army (to Wilkinson's horror), marched most of the troops back to Sackets Harbor. The remainder went with Wilkinson to Plattsburgh.

8

FIRE AND SWORD ON THE FRONTIER

When most of the American army had withdrawn to Sackets Harbor and Plattsburgh, the British had a chance to pounce on the unguarded Niagara frontier. Strong forces arrived from Kingston under the command of Lieutenant General Gordon Drummond, a Canadian with long years of service in the British army. General McClure, who had taken command at Fort George when Scott joined Wilkinson's expedition, suddenly found his small garrison menaced by swarms of Indians and British troops. His militia had gone home, and McClure decided to abandon Fort George and take his little force of less than 100 men across the river to Fort Niagara.

Deep snow lay on the ground and the temperature was near zero when McClure put the torch to the nearby village of Newark to "deprive the advancing British forces of shelter." Commenting on this act, American historian Benson J. Lossing, who interviewed survivors of the War of 1812 during the 1860's, wrote: "The inhabitants had been given only a few hours' warning; and, with little food and clothing, a large number of helpless women and children were driven from their homes into the wintry air, homeless wanderers. Oh! it was a cruel act. War is always cruel, but this was more cruel than necessity demanded. It excited hot indignation and the spirit of vengeance, which soon caused the hand of retaliation to work fearfully. It provoked the commission of great injury to American property and left a stain upon the American character."

A British force commanded by Colonel John Murray saw the flames of Newark staining the sky and advanced rapidly to attack McClure. Murray was too late to catch the Americans, but his swift advance caused McClure to leave so quickly that he failed to blow up the fort or the barracks. The Americans also left behind tents for 1,500 men, along with artillery and ammunition. The British now had additional shelter and supplies for their campaign—a fact that made McClure's burning of Newark even more cruel and stupid.

General Drummond observed the ruins of Newark and told his officers to retaliate "by fire and sword." On December 19, 1813, Colonel Murray's British regulars, trailed by 600 Indians, stealthily approached Fort Niagara. Despite warnings that the enemy was near, someone had left the gate of the fort open. The fort's commander was with his family in a house three miles away. The British charged into the fort and bayoneted 65 men before allowing the remaining 300 to surrender. Then, Drummond set his Indian allies to pillaging and burning. Between December 19 and January 1, 1814, the American settlements at Buffalo, Black Rock, Lewiston, Youngstown, Manchester, Schlosser, and Tuscarora Village were reduced to piles of ashes. A strip of land 36 miles long and 12 miles wide on the American side of the Niagara River was burned out.

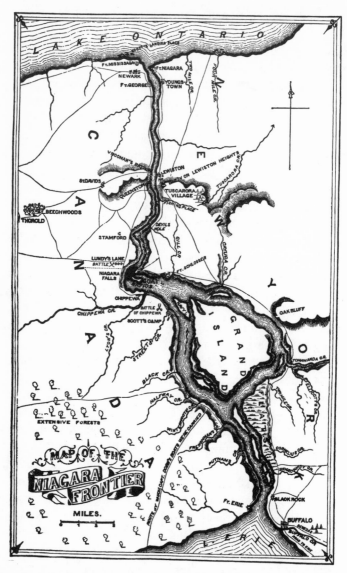

After American forces had been withdrawn from the Niagara frontier during Wilkinson's advance down the St. Lawrence River, the British put this area to the torch and destroyed Lewiston, Tuscarora Village, Schlosser, Black Rock, and Buffalo—a strip of land 36 miles long.

In Buffalo one woman stubbornly refused to flee. "I can't do it," she told a neighbor. "Here is all I have in the world, and I will stay and defend it." She did defend her home, not by force but by kindness, and the Indians spared her life and property. Another woman also refused to flee, but she resisted the Indians and was killed and scalped. Before the Indians arrived, she told her son Henry, who had served in the militia, to run. "Henry, you have fought against the British. You must run. They will take you prisoner. I am a woman. They'll not harm me." He fled to the woods and escaped the British and Indians.

The bitter condemnation of General McClure by both sides and the savage retaliation of the British caused Sir George Prevost to promise an end to this total war against civilians. In a proclamation issued on January 12, 1814, Prevost said he would not continue the policy that was "so revolting to my own feelings . . ." unless the future conduct of the American government compelled him to retaliate.

Soon after this proclamation, Colonel John B. Campbell led an expedition across Lake Erie. He burned two villages in Upper Canada, and coolly wrote General Brown that "this expedition was undertaken by me without orders and upon my own responsibility." He also added that he probably would burn another Canadian town if he got the chance. General Brown put an X through that part of the letter and sent the original to Prevost. He hoped to convince the governor general that the American government condemned Campbell's act. A court-martial found Colonel Campbell guilty merely of an "error of judgment," but it sternly declared that any retaliation against the enemy could be ordered only by the government. Campbell did not hear the verdict of the court because he was killed four days before it was announced.

Angered by Campbell's expedition, Prevost ignored

Brown's explanation. He ordered Admiral Sir Alexander Cochrane, commander of the British warships blockading the American coast, to burn any coastal towns that British landing parties could reach.

9

AN OVERDUE
HOUSECLEANING

When Secretary of War Armstrong was not busy trying to mastermind a campaign, he was a reasonably efficient official. He had done much to get Congress to pass a law on March 3, 1813, that gave the secretary of war the aid of a general staff of trained officers. Instead of having to depend on a few ink-stained clerks, the secretary had the advice and assistance of an inspector general, quartermaster general, a commissary general, a paymaster, and an assistant topographical engineer.

Armstrong also made progress weeding out generals who were misfits and replacing them with younger men. In June 1812, the army had eight generals whose average age was 60 years. Two years later, every one of them had either been dismissed from the service or been sent to a quiet area where he couldn't do any harm. In the first five months of 1814, nine generals were appointed or promoted to a higher rank. Their average age was 36, a drop of 24 years in 36 months. The new major generals were Jacob Brown, 38; George Izard, 37; and Andrew Jackson, 46. Among the new brigadier generals were Winfield Scott, only 27; Alexander Macomb, 31; and Edmund P. Gaines, 37.

General Wilkinson who, with Wade Hampton and Morgan Lewis, was not one of Secretary Armstrong's wise appointments, was still around stirring up trouble early in 1814. From his Plattsburgh headquarters Wilkinson wrote Armstrong, demanding a court-martial to fix the blame for the failure of the Montreal expedition. Speaking of Armstrong to Dearborn, Wilkinson said: "Good God! I am astonished at the man's audacity, when he must be sensible to the power I have over him." Here, again, Wilkinson would seem to have been indulging in a dream brought on by laudanum.

While his letter demanding a court-martial was on its way to Washington, Wilkinson decided on one more gamble to win honors. He would strike from Plattsburgh and take Montreal before the British knew what was going on. As an afterthought, he contended that his expedition was vital to keep the British from sending troops to the western frontier, something they weren't planning to do at that time.

Wilkinson's small army of 4,000 men crossed the Canadian border on March 30, 1814, and marched toward the La Colle River. It was at this stream that Dearborn's invasion of Canada had come to an inglorious end in 1812. The Americans reached the river and found that the British had fortified La Colle Mill, a stone building with walls 18 inches thick. The British garrison was small, about 200 men, but they were regulars. Wilkinson's artillerymen tried to drag an 18-pound cannon forward to batter down the walls of the mill. But the ground, which was half-flooded by melting snow, was too soft to hold the gun. A 12-pound cannon and a small mortar finally were placed 250 yards from the mill. They banged away for several hours, but their shots bounced off the stone walls of the mill. Then reinforcements reached the British defenders, and they made several determined attacks on the American lines. After two hours of fighting, Wilkinson had had enough. He ordered a retreat. His invasion of Canada had lasted a day and cost the Americans 13 killed, 128 wounded, and 13 missing. The British lost 11 killed, 46 wounded, and 4 missing.

The War Department finally relieved Wilkinson of his command, and he later faced a court-martial on charges of neglect of duty, drunkenness, and willful lying. For the third time, Wilkinson was put on trial by the army, and for the third time, he was acquitted. But never again was he allowed to command an American army. Critics summed up Wilkinson's career neatly: "He never won a battle or lost a court-martial."

10

BROWN AND SCOTT BUILD AN ARMY

On February 28, 1814, Secretary of War Armstrong wrote a letter to Major General Jacob Brown, commander of the Army of the North. Armstrong was back in the business of planning a campaign—a job he should have left to other men. His letter contained two orders. One sent Brown's division of 3,000 men and Commodore Chauncey's fleet against the main British base at Kingston. The other order appeared to call for a campaign on the Niagara frontier. Armstrong intended Brown to fake a punch at Niagara to confuse the British, and then launch his main attack at Kingston. But the wording of Armstrong's orders was so obscure that they wound up merely confusing Brown.

While Brown was puzzling over Armstrong's letter, Chauncey stepped in and convinced him that their land and naval forces were too weak to attack Kingston. So Brown started marching his troops toward the Niagara frontier. Brown was at Geneva, New York, when General Gaines convinced him that Armstrong really wanted the army to attack Kingston. Brown agreed and hurried back to Sackets Harbor, "the most unhappy man alive." But Chauncey flatly refused to give naval support for an attack on Kingston until he had completed work on a new warship. So Brown went back to the Niagara frontier to make the best of things.

When Armstrong learned of his return to Niagara, he wrote a soothing letter to Brown on March 20, saying that Brown had mistaken his meaning. The order to attack Niagara was "merely a mask for the operation against Kingston. If you hazard anything by this mistake, correct it promptly by returning to your post [at Sackets Harbor]. If on the other hand, you left the Harbor with a competent force for its defense, go on and prosper. Good consequences are sometimes the result of mistakes."

Disturbed by Secretary Armstrong's confusing orders, Brown left General Scott in command of the troops at Buffalo and went back to Sackets Harbor to assure himself that it was safe. During the winter, the British and American naval forces had been engaged in a shipbuilding race. In April 1814, Commodore Yeo launched two ships of 58 and 40 guns. These ships gave Yeo control of Lake Ontario, and he then set out to cripple Chauncey's shipbuilding program. But instead of attacking Sackets Harbor, Yeo sent his fleet to destroy the American supply depot at Oswego, New York. There, the guns, cables, and stores for Chauncey's fleet were collected to be carried by water to Sackets Harbor. On May 6, the British captured Oswego and burned the fort. But most of the supplies for Chauncey's fleet had been moved inland and were not destroyed.

Yeo then clamped a naval blockade on Sackets Harbor that threatened to bring Chauncey's building program to a halt. Light equipment could be carried by land, but not the big guns weighing many tons, and anchor cables that were 22 inches thick and hundreds of feet long. The narrow, muddy roads between Oswego and Sackets Harbor could not handle such heavy equipment. Chauncey gave Captain Melancthon Woolsey the job of getting the guns and cables to Sackets Harbor. Woolsey organized convoys of boats that carried the supplies along the shore of the lake at night as far as Sandy Creek. Then the boats went up that stream to a point three miles from Sackets Harbor. From there, the guns and cables could be dragged to the American naval base.

On May 29, one of Yeo's ships spotted Woolsey's convoy moving into Sandy Creek. Yeo ordered Captain Stephen Popham to take 200 seamen and marines and go after the convoy. Captain Popham had been the hero of a similar raid on the French coast a few years earlier, and he expected no trouble from the Americans. But Woolsey had 130 riflemen and 100 friendly Indians concealed along both banks of Sandy Creek. They ambushed Popham's men, killing 18, wounding 50, and capturing the rest, including the embarrassed Popham. The British not only lost more than 100 skilled seamen, which were hard to replace, but Chauncey got the guns and cables he needed. Early in June, shortly after the Sandy Creek defeat, Yeo ended his blockade of Sackets Harbor.

In April, President Madison and his advisers had studied Armstrong's plan for another invasion across the Niagara River. General Brown's troops were to cross the river, capture Fort Erie, sweep northward along the left bank of the river through Queenston, and recapture Fort George. Then, Brown would recross the river and take back Fort Niagara on the American shore. At the mouth of the Niagara, Brown was to be met by Chauncey's fleet. Protected and supplied by the fleet, Brown would march on Burlington Heights and drive the British out of the peninsula between Lake Erie and Lake Ontario.

The British army facing Brown was composed of about 2,300 men, including some Indians, all commanded by Brigadier General Phineas Riall, an Irish officer of uncertain ability. But at Burlington Heights and York were reinforcements that could increase Riall's army to 4,000.

News from Europe made it clear that any move by Brown would have to be made quickly. The British and their allies had taken Paris on March 31, 1814, and in May, Napoleon abdicated and went into exile on the Island of Elba. Immediate plans were made to send 14 regiments of the Duke of Wellington's best troops to Canada. This force was expected to reach Quebec not later than August. So Governor General Prevost could afford in July to send every regular in the St. Lawrence area to the Niagara frontier.

Wrangling between Armstrong and Secretary of the Navy William Jones delayed final approval of the Niagara campaign until June 7. Armstrong wrote Brown on June 10, telling him what to do. First, he told Brown that the secretary of the navy did not believe Chauncey would be ready to aid him before July 15. But Armstrong saw no reason for Brown to wait for Chauncey. He wrote: "To give immediate occupation to your troops, and to prevent their blood from stagnating, why not take Fort Erie and its garrison? . . . Push forward a corps to seize the bridge at Chippewa and be governed by circumstances in either stopping there or going farther. . . . If the enemy concentrates his whole force on this line, as I think he will, it will not exceed two thousand men." Unfortunately, Armstrong didn't have very good sources of information on the British strength.

Brown was in Buffalo with his troops when Armstrong's orders reached him. Refusing to worry at that time about hints that Chauncey might drag his feet, Brown began making plans for his campaign. Hoping to strengthen his army, Brown called for volunteers to be commanded by Brigadier General Peter B. Porter, a War Hawk member of Congress in 1812. On June 21, Brown finally wrote Chauncey a sharply worded letter complaining of not hearing from him. He also challenged the navy to meet the army at Fort George by July 10. The letter showed that Brown did not consider Chauncey any more dependable than Wilkinson. Brown was to get no help from Chauncey, and Porter could collect only 700 Pennsylvania volunteers. Brown's whole force numbered less than 3,500 men, but among them were two brigades of regular army troops. It was on the regiments in these brigades that Brown counted. Although these regiments were disbanded after the war and their honors were won in a short campaign of less than four months, they should be identified here.

The First Brigade, commanded by Brigadier General Scott, consisted of: 9th Regiment, commanded by Major Henry Leavenworth, recruited in Massachusetts; 11th Regiment, commanded by Major John McNeil, recruited in Vermont; 22nd Regiment, commanded by Colonel Hugh Brady, recruited in Pennsylvania; 25th Regiment, commanded by Major Thomas S. Jesup, recruited in Connecticut. This brigade had 1,384 officers and men present for duty on July 1, 1814.

The Second Brigade, commanded by Brigadier General Eleazar W. Ripley, consisted of: 21st Regiment, commanded by Major James Miller, recruited in Massachusetts; 23rd Regiment, commanded by Major Daniel McFarland, recruited in New York. This brigade had 1,027 officers and men present for duty on July 1, 1814. Although the governors of the New England states gave little support to the war, a majority of the men in Brown's two brigades were from New England.

The artillery was commanded by Major Jacob Hindman and Captain Nathan Towson, and Captain Samuel D. Harris led a small squadron of cavalry.

The militia brigade, commanded by General Porter, consisted of 700 Pennsylvania volunteers. Attached to Porter's brigade were about 600 Indian warriors of the Six Nations.

They had been rallied by Red Jacket, the great Seneca orator and chief.

Brown's regulars did not always deserve that name. When these troops reached Buffalo in March 1814, most of them were as untrained and undisciplined as the rawest militia. While Brown was keeping an eye on things at Sackets Harbor, he had General Scott form a "camp of instruction" for the troops at Buffalo. Determined to avoid the death and disease he had seen under Wilkinson in Louisiana, Scott put his men in tents on well-drained land and strictly enforced rules of sanitation. Then Scott hauled out his textbook on military drill and tactics and began to train soldiers. He acted as his own drill sergeant and first instructed the officers of each regiment. From March until June the officers went out and taught their men to march properly, deploy, fire, and use the bayonet. Scott's methods recalled the painstaking work of Baron von Steuben, who had turned Washington's raw recruits at Valley Forge into tough, disciplined regulars.

Major Jesup wrote that he "began, under the orders of General Scott, a course of instruction, and kept my command under arms from seven to ten hours a day. A similar course was pursued by the chiefs of other corps. The consequence was, that when we took the field in July, our corps maneuvered in action and under the fire of the enemy's artillery with the accuracy of parade."

Many of the men grumbled and some tried to desert, but Scott was satisfied with their progress. "If, of such materials, I do not make the best Army now in service by the 1st of June, I will agree to be dismissed from the service."

On July 2, Brown completed his plans for the attack on Fort Erie. Scott's brigade was to set out and cross the Niagara River from Buffalo, landing a mile north of the fort, while Ripley's brigade was to cross at Black Rock and land the same distance south of the fort. The movement was to be completed before dawn of the 3rd, and Fort Erie was to be immediately attacked. The evening of the 2nd, Ripley objected to the plans for the attack and wanted it delayed. He believed that his brigade, which was smaller than Scott's, would have to do the heaviest fighting, so he asked for more troops. Afraid that a delay would give Riall time to reinforce Fort Erie, Brown tried to convince Ripley that his force was strong enough for the job ahead. Ripley then angrily said that he did not think Fort Erie could be taken and offered his resignation. Brown refused it and told Ripley to carry out his orders. Defenders of Ripley say he was a brave soldier but a cautious man who suffered by comparison with those hard-headed fighters, Brown and Scott.

Scott's brigade crossed the river in the darkness and was ready to attack at dawn. But it was broad daylight before the reluctant Ripley had his men in their boats. Brown ordered Scott to attack without waiting, and it turned out that Ripley's tardiness made no difference because Fort Erie was weakly defended. After a short skirmish that cost the lives of four Americans, the British garrison of 200 men surrendered.

Hearing of the threat to Fort Erie, General Riall had hurried forward with reinforcements of 1,500 regulars and 600 militia and Indians at eight o'clock in the morning of July 3. When he got the word that Fort Erie had fallen, Riall halted at Chippewa, north of the fort, and waited for Brown's next move. If Brown had delayed his attack, as Ripley had urged, Fort Erie might not have been taken. Or, at least, its capture would have cost the lives of a good many Americans.

The next day, July 4, Scott's brigade and Captain Towson's artillery were ordered to advance toward Chippewa. Scott marched northward along the Canadian side of the Niagara River. On the way, Major Jesup's 25th Regiment met the British 100th Regiment commanded by the Marquis of

Tweeddale. There followed a nasty running fight for 16 miles, and the British wound up panting on the other side of the Chippewa River. Observing the gray uniforms worn by Scott's brigade, the Marquis had thought these troops were "only Buffalo militia." He could account for their surprising fighting spirit only by the fact that they were celebrating the anniversary of American independence and were all fired up because of it.

A shortage of cloth for American uniforms had led to the Marquis's mistake. While his brigade was training at Buffalo, Scott wrote to the quartermaster for a supply of new clothing for his regulars. The quartermaster said that blue cloth, such as was used in the army, could not be obtained owing to the blockade and the lack of manufacturers in the country. There was, said the quartermaster, a quantity of gray cloth in Philadelphia. Scott ordered it made into uniforms for his men.

Discovering that the enemy was strongly posted beyond the Chippewa, Scott fell back to a position behind Street's Creek. At about midnight, the rest of Brown's army arrived.

The British and American forces now were only about a mile apart. Between them was a plain, flanked on the east by the Niagara River and on the west by a dense forest.

Accepting the Marquis of Tweeddale's word that he was facing Buffalo militia, General Riall boldly prepared to attack Brown's army. British scouts and Indians occupied the forest on the American left flank and began harassing the camp guards and outposts. Early in the afternoon of July 5, Scott ordered Porter's brigade of militia and Indians to clear the enemy from the forest. Porter's force drove the British and Indians back almost to the Chippewa River. Then, the Americans and Indians found themselves facing the whole British army, which was crossing the river. Porter's brigade fell back in great confusion.

The alert, tireless Brown was at the front and saw Porter's men running. He also saw a huge cloud of dust to the north and correctly surmised that Riall's army was advancing toward the plain in front of Street's Creek. Brown immediately sent an officer with an order for General Ripley to bring his brigade forward. He then rode toward General Scott's headquarters. At this moment, Scott was preparing to cross Street's Creek and assemble his force on the plain, which, unknown to him, was already being occupied by the British. Scott had rested his men in the morning and given them a good dinner at noon to celebrate the Fourth of July one day late. Then he ordered a parade to sweat out the food and drink the men had consumed and "to keep them in breath." Because of the thick brush lining Street's Creek, Scott could not see the British on the plain. Now, General Brown rode by at full gallop and shouted: "You will have a battle!" Confident that Scott could handle his job, Brown rode on to hurry Ripley's brigade into action. Scott calmly told his officers that he did not believe there were even 300 British around, and then led his troops across the creek.

As Scott's troops reached the plain, the British artillery began hammering them. Scott quickly recovered from his surprise and snapped out orders to his officers. Despite the deadly fire from the enemy, the American regulars coolly formed a line of battle. If a man was hit, the line immediately closed up in perfect order, not missing a step. The long hours of drill that Scott had ordered at Buffalo were paying off in this crisis. Watching the gray-clad Americans maneuver under fire, the startled Riall shouted: "Those are regulars, by God!"

Scott ordered Major Jesup's 25th Regiment to protect the left flank, which had been exposed by the rout of Porter's brigade. The 9th and part of the 22nd, commanded by Major Leavenworth, covered the right flank. The 11th Regiment under Major McNeil occupied the center of Scott's line. Captain Towson's annoyingly accurate guns began dropping shells into the British lines, blowing up an ammunition wagon and causing the enemy to hestitate.

Then the whole American line advanced, halted, fired, and advanced again until it was within 80 paces of the British. There, within sound of the great falls of the Niagara, the Americans and British slugged it out in a face-to-face battle. General Riall now proved to be an unskillful handler of troops, and gaps began to appear in the British line. Scott quickly saw an opportunity to hit those gaps. Riding over to Major McNeil's 11th Regiment, Scott shouted: "The enemy say we are good at long shot, but cannot stand the cold iron! I call upon the Eleventh instantly to give the lie to that slander! Charge!"

McNeil's men ripped the British line apart with their bayonets. Major Leavenworth and Major Jesup also led their troops in charges that swept the enemy aside. The British regulars fled, hotly pursued by the Americans. The stubborn Riall courageously rode toward the Americans, seemingly wanting to be killed, but his staff officers persuaded him to leave the field. The British didn't stop running till they were back at the Chippewa, where they removed the planks from the bridge and posted artillery to halt Scott's troops. Since Ripley's brigade did not arrive until the battle was over, the American brigade that beat Riall actually was smaller than the British force—1,300 against 1,500.

The Americans lost 61 killed, 255 wounded, and 19 missing; the British, 236 killed, 320 wounded, and 46 missing. A comparison of losses showed that the American musket fire had been highly efficient. When loading, Scott's regulars had placed over each musket ball three buckshots which scattered with deadly effect. The casualties among British officers had been particularly heavy. One regiment alone had two officers killed and 20 wounded.

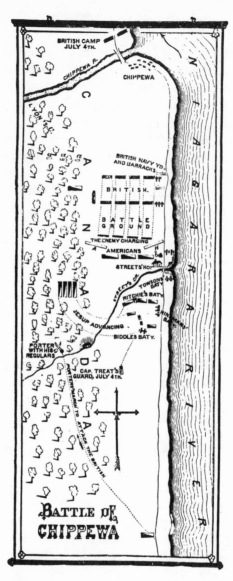

This map of the Battle of Chippewa shows the position of the British and American forces before Major McNeil's regiment made its decisive charge.

American historian Henry Adams commented: "The Battle of Chippewa was the only occasion during the war when equal bodies of regular troops met face to face, in extended lines on an open plain in broad daylight, without advantage of position; and never again after that combat was an army of American regulars beaten by British troops. Small as the affair was, and unimportant in military results, it gave the United States Army a character and pride it had never before possessed."

News of Chippewa cheered the nation at a time when people were worrying about reports of the arrival in Canada of Wellington's veterans. Brown and Scott were honored throughout the country, and volunteers began flocking to the army. In this report to Secretary of War Armstrong, Brown wrote: "Brigadier General Scott is entitled to the highest praise our country can bestow; to him more than any other man I am indebted for the victory of the 5th of July. His brigade covered itself with glory."

The gray uniforms worn by the cadets at West Point honor Scott's gray-clad brigade at Chippewa.

Although some British writers quibbled and grumbled over Riall's defeat, many of them generously acknowledged the fighting spirit of the American regulars. One writer declared: "The important fact is that we have now got an enemy who fights as bravely as ourselves. For some time, the Americans cut no figure on land. They have now proved to us that they only wanted time to acquire a little discipline. They have proved to us what they are made of; that they are the same sort of men as those who captured whole armies under Burgoyne and Cornwallis; that they are neither to be frightened nor silenced."

While the combative Scott was preparing to follow the British across the Chippewa, a heavy rain swept over the battlefield. At this time, two of Scott's officers returned to report that the British position was too strong to be attacked on the evening of the 5th. So Scott marched his troops back across the now muddy plain to their camp along Street's Creek.

Brown was impatient to advance because he hoped to meet Chauncey's fleet at the mouth of the Niagara River on July 10. He was convinced, however, that a frontal attack on the British at Chippewa bridge would be too costly in lives. So Brown sent a scouting party to hunt a place to cross the Chippewa west of the enemy camp. The scouts returned to report that an old timber road led to the Chippewa at the mouth of Lyons Creek. Brown went out to see for himself, was satisfied that it was adequate, and immediately planned to attack. Wanting to give Ripley's brigade a chance to win honors too, Brown ordered him to cross the Chippewa at Lyons Creek on July 7 and attack the flank of Riall's army. But Ripley, as usual, offered objections to the plan and delayed his march. Brown hurried up to take command of the brigade from the foot-dragging Ripley. British scouts now discovered Brown's movement, and Riall hastily retreated to Queenston. When the American army pushed on toward Queenston, Riall sent troops to strengthen Forts George and Niagara and retreated west toward Burlington Heights to await reinforcements.

Brown camped at Queenston on July 10. From the heights, he anxiously scanned the waters of Lake Ontario, only seven miles away, hoping to see the sails of Chauncey's fleet. To take Fort George, Brown would need heavy siege guns and more troops and supplies, which Chauncey was supposed to bring him. Above all, he needed the fleet to keep the British from bringing troops across Lake Ontario from York to reinforce Riall. But Chauncey's fleet never showed up. On July 13, an angry Brown wrote to Chauncey: "I do not doubt my ability to meet the enemy in the field and to march in any direction over his country, your fleet carrying for me the necessary supplies. We can threaten Forts George

and Niagara and carry Burlington Heights and York, and
proceed to Kingston and carry that place. All accounts represent the force of the enemy at Kingston as very little. Sir
James [Yeo] will not fight. For God's sake, let me see you.
I have looked for your fleet with the greatest anxiety since
the 10th."

Unfortunately, Chauncey was ill, and he was not willing
to let anyone else use his fleet to fight Yeo or carry supplies
to Brown. A cautious, meticulous man, Chauncey refused to
move until every gun, cable, bolt, and rope were in place. He
ignored Brown's call for help. When the secretary of the navy
complained of Chauncey's inaction, the commodore wrote:
"The squadron has been prevented being earlier fitted for sea
because of the delay in obtaining blocks and ironwork." The
shocked secretary replied that the excuse about the ships' need-
ing ironwork was "so extraordinary" that he was compelled
to report "the extreme anxiety and astonishment" of President
Madison.

On July 23, Brown received word from General Gaines,
commanding at Sackets Harbor, that Chauncey was ill and
his fleet was not ready to leave. This bad news was followed by
reports that Riall had received reinforcements and had advanced from Burlington Heights to Fifteen-Mile Creek, only
13 miles from the American camp. More troops, commanded
by General Drummond, were also on the march to join Riall.
The tough Drummond, commander in chief of forces in Upper
Canada, had won honors when his troops captured Fort Niagara in December of 1813. Brown called a council of
officers, who decided that the army had to have supplies and
was too weak to stay at Queenston. There was nothing to do
but fall back, get supplies from the village of Schlosser on the
American side of the river, and then make a stand against the
British.

Before the retreat began, troops of General Porter's

militia, under the command of Colonel Isaac W. Stone, plundered and burned the village of St. David's near Queenston, on July 19. Stone was court-martialed, convicted, and promptly dismissed from the service by General Brown. Major McFarland of the 23rd Regiment, who was to die in battle at Lundy's Lane a few days later, wrote his family: "The militia have burnt several private dwelling houses, and on the 19th, burnt the village of St. David's. . . . This was done within three miles of the camp. . . . I never before witnessed such a scene; and had not the commanding officer, Colonel Stone, been disgraced and sent out of the army, I should have resigned my commission."

In his effort to enforce discipline in the army, General Brown had earlier taken prompt and harsh action against an officer whom he had highly esteemed. During the early morning skirmishing before the Battle of Chippewa, Captain Joseph Treat commanded a picket guard of 40 men and a patrol of 10. According to reports received by Brown, Treat "retired disgracefully, leaving a wounded man on the ground." For this offense, Brown ordered Treat, on the spot, to retire from the army. In his report of the incident, General Brown recommended the dismissal of Treat and one of his lieutenants from the service. "This punishment," said Brown, "though severe, was just, and at the moment indispensable. It had the happiest effect upon the army." Brown felt that Captain Treat had failed in his first responsibility as an officer—to look after his men.

On the day of his disgrace, Captain Treat volunteered to fight as a private in the ranks. Major Vose of the 21st Regiment, who still had full confidence in Treat, asked the captain to take command of a platoon during the Battle of Chippewa. He declined, but fought courageously in the ranks. Captain Treat later appeared before General Brown and demanded a court-martial. It was granted, but the court did not meet for many months due to delays caused by the continuing campaign on the Niagara frontier. On May 8, 1815, the court finally announced its verdict: "After mature deliberation on the testimony deduced, the court find the accused, Captain Joseph Treat, not guilty of the charge or specification preferred against him, and do honorably acquit him." The finding of the court was approved by General Brown.

On July 24, 1814, the retreating American army was back at Chippewa. It was followed by the British, commanded by General Riall. Rumors then circulated that another British force commanded by General Drummond had crossed to the American side of the Niagara River at Lewiston. This was jolting news because the vital supply base at Schlosser was near Lewiston. Furthermore, Brown's army was in danger of being trapped between two British forces. Another general might have decided to get out of the Niagara region as quickly as possible. But Brown was in no mood to order another retreat. He decided upon a bold move to upset the British commanders. He would send Scott's brigade forward to attack Riall and force Drummond to bring his troops back from the American side of the Niagara River. But as it happened, Drummond had sent only a small detachment to raid Lewiston, and it had been repulsed by American militia. Drummond and the major part of his force were still marching full speed to join Riall, who was at Lundy's Lane, about a mile from Niagara Falls.

11

"I'LL TRY, SIR"

At five o'clock in the afternoon of July 25, General Scott's brigade, with Captain Towson's artillery, crossed Chippewa bridge and marched toward Niagara Falls, whose roaring waters could be plainly heard. The Battle of Chippewa and three weeks of campaigning had reduced Scott's command to around 1,000 men. As his troops emerged from a woods, they suddenly came upon Riall's army, drawn up in battle order in Lundy's Lane, a highway running from the Niagara River to the head of Lake Ontario. By this time Riall had been joined by Drummond, who had brought some of Wellington's veterans, and the British force numbered over 1,700 men. Scott was in a tight spot. His men were already under heavy artillery fire, and standing still would be fatal. A retreat would be equally dangerous because the men might be thrown into confusion while trying to cross the narrow Chippewa bridge. Besides, Scott was not the kind of officer who liked to think about retreating. Immediately, Scott determined to attack Riall and make him think he was facing the whole American army. Scott shouted to his men: "We must fight! No retreat!"

The British line was in a crescent shape, the wings being thrown ahead of the artillery, which was in the center on a hill. As Scott boldly led his regulars against the British, his sharp eye spotted a heavy growth of brush between the left end of the enemy line and the river. He ordered Major Jesup's 25th Regiment to move through the brush and attempt to get behind the British line while Scott's other regiments hit the British center. While the 9th, 11th, and 22nd Regiments kept up a heavy musket fire, Jesup's forces managed to get behind the British. There, they captured General Riall, who had been wounded, and several of his staff officers. Then, British reinforcements threatened to overwhelm Jesup's troops, but they fought their way through the British and got back to the American line.

From seven until nine o'clock, Scott's troops repeatedly charged the British center, were hurled back, and charged again. The 11th and 22nd Regiments lost 230 men, killed, wounded, and missing—more than half their number. When the 11th Regiment faltered, Major McNeil spurred his horse in front of the troops. A huge man, six feet six, with a voice to match, McNeil roared threats and entreaties until he got his men back into the fight. McNeil's horse was killed and he was wounded in both legs, but he stayed in action until he collapsed from loss of blood. Colonel Brady of the 22nd also was severely wounded, so Major Leavenworth of the 9th took command of the remnants of the 11th and 22nd.

Scott's exhausted force of no more than 600 men was ready to collapse when Brown came up on the run with Ripley's and Porter's brigades. The American army was also strengthened by Colonel Robert Nicholas's 1st Regiment of

150 men, which had crossed the Niagara that afternoon, and by artillery commanded by Captains Ritchie and Biddle.

Brown quickly realized that Scott's troops had to be given a rest. He ordered Ripley and Porter to form a new line of battle with their brigades. In the smoke and darkness and confusion, the cool, keen-eyed Brown also saw clearly that the key to the enemy's position was the battery of heavy guns on the hill. The Americans could not hope to win unless those guns were taken. Turning to Colonel Miller of the 21st Regiment, Brown said: "Colonel, take your regiment, storm that work, and take it."

"I'll try, sir," said Miller and he hurried over to his men. As Miller's troops started to advance, Colonel Nicholas's 1st Regiment, which was supposed to draw the enemy's attention away from Miller's 21st Regiment, fell back in confusion. Miller paid no attention to the collapse of the 1st. His 450 men moved up the hill, mostly concealed by a rail fence, along which was a thick growth of brush. General Ripley now led the 23rd Regiment up the hill to support Miller. Ripley's men ran into a heavy enemy fire and were driven back, but Ripley rallied them and got them back into action.

Miller's men reached a point within 40 feet of the battery of guns on the hill. They could see the gunners with their lighted matches, waiting for the command to fire. Following the whispered orders of Miller and his officers, the men fired a volley that killed or wounded every British gunner and then charged into the middle of the battery. The British force that was posted to guard the battery fired a deadly volley and went for Miller's men with bayonets. The regulars of the 21st held their ground and beat back the charge. Another British unit advanced to within 20 paces of Miller's troops. A sheet of flame flashed up and down the lines as both sides fired volley after volley. Slowly, the British began to fall back. Now,

Ripley led 300 men of the 23rd Regiment against the British flank, shattered it with musket fire, and drove it from the hill.

When the firing died down, Ripley's two regiments held the hill and the whole length of Lundy's Lane. Brown was sure that Drummond, who had received more reinforcements, was not going to quit yet. He brought Porter's brigade in on the left, and placed Towson's and Ritchie's guns on either side of Ripley's two regiments. Jesup's 25th Regiment was put on the right flank. Major Leavenworth, commanding the remnants of the 9th, 11th, and 22nd Regiments, formed a second line behind the captured British guns.

As Brown had expected, Drummond quickly hurled fresh troops into a charge to retake his guns. The American and British lines exchanged fire at a distance of less than 12 yards for over 20 minutes. In the darkness, the men aimed at the flash of the muskets. One of Ripley's officers said, "You could see the figures on their buttons by the light of the guns." The British took it as long as they could and then fell back. But the red-coated regulars would not quit. Many of them had fought for Wellington, and they were not used to being treated this way. When Drummond ordered another attack, they did not hesitate. They charged three more times during the next two hours, only to be driven back by the deadly musket fire of the Americans. By midnight, Drummond and his troops had had enough. The British commander pulled his force back toward Queenston.

By this time, Scott had been carried from the field with a badly mangled shoulder. Brown had been shot through the hip and his side was severely bruised by a shell fragment. Ripley, who had sat calmly on his horse 10 paces behind his line, had two bullet holes in his hat but was unhurt. Among the American officers killed were Major McFarland of the 23rd Regiment and Captain Abraham F. Hull of the 9th

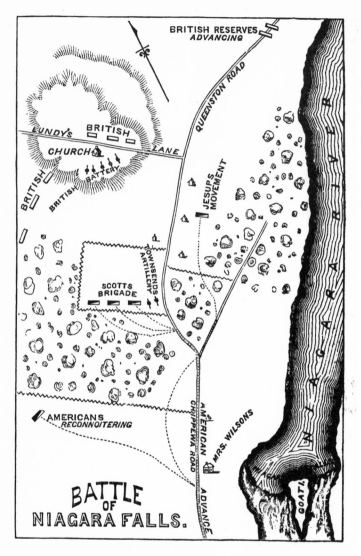

This map of the Battle of Lundy's Lane (also called the Battle of Niagara Falls) shows, to the right, the flanking movement of Major Jesup's regiment, which resulted in the capture of the British commander, General Riall.

Regiment. It was his father, General William Hull, who had meekly surrendered at Detroit in 1812.

The Battle of Lundy's Lane, or Niagara Falls, lasted five hours and was, for the numbers engaged, the most savage in the history of the United States Army. The Americans lost 171 killed, 572 wounded, and 110 missing. The British lost 84 killed, 559 wounded, 193 missing, and 42 captured.

Afterward Drummond always insisted that his army had fought 5,000 Americans, and the British government commended him for his "gallant stand against superior forces." But Brown never had more than 2,000 men in action.

In his report, Drummond admitted that the Americans had fought with great courage: "In so determined a manner were the attacks directed against our guns that the artillerymen were bayoneted by the enemy in the act of loading, and the muzzles of the enemy guns were advanced within a few yards of ours."

Other British officers who had faced Napoleon's tough veterans said they had "never seen such determined charges as were made by the Americans." They also called Miller's seizure of the British guns "the most desperate thing we ever saw or heard of." When Brown met Miller after the attack, he said, "You have immortalized yourself! My dear fellow, my heart ached for you when I gave you the order, but I knew that it was the only thing that would save us."

Miller's reply to Brown's order, "I'll try, sir," became the motto of the 5th Regiment, the successor to the 21st when the army was reorganized after the war.

The Battle of Lundy's Lane was said to have doubled the strength of the American army by giving it confidence in its generals and in itself. And the memory of Lundy's Lane encouraged people during the dark days when British armies occupied Washington and hammered at the defenses of Baltimore in August, and threatened Plattsburgh in September.

12

"I CAN BLOW THEM ALL TO HELL"

As Brown was being carried from the field of battle after the victory at Lundy's Lane, he directed Ripley, now in command, to march the army back to Chippewa, where the men could get water. But he also ordered Ripley to march again at dawn for Lundy's Lane and get the cannon that had been captured. The lack of horses and drag ropes had prevented the Americans from moving the guns that night.

Because of the disorganization of many regiments that had lost most of their officers, Ripley could not get the army ready to march until nine the next morning. When he neared Lundy's Lane, he found that Drummond had returned, recovered his guns, and taken a strong defensive position. Although Ripley's force was small, Drummond was in no mood to take another whack at it. Ripley marched back to camp and reported to Brown, who exploded angrily. Brown decided not to trust Ripley with command of the army and immediately sent a message to Brigadier General Gaines telling him to come up from Sackets Harbor and take command of the army on the Niagara frontier.

The officers now debated whether to stay at the Chippewa River or retreat. The cautious Ripley, in command until Gaines arrived, recommended a retreat, and on July 26 ordered the army to march to Fort Erie. That evening, Brown and Scott were taken across the river to recover from their wounds. Brown stayed at Buffalo and Scott was taken to Williamsville, Wyoming County, New York. There, he met the wounded General Riall and the men became friends. Scott's wound was so severe that he was kept out of action for the rest of the war.

Shortly after arriving at Fort Erie, Ripley announced his intention of abandoning that post and retreating to the American side of the river. His officers objected violently, and Ripley went to Buffalo to confer with Brown, who angrily told him to return to Fort Erie and strengthen its defenses. Brown then wrote a report to Secretary of War Armstrong, implying that Ripley was wanting in either courage or ability. Later, Brown regretted this criticism and said of Ripley: "General Brown entertained no doubt of the intelligence or bravery of General Ripley," but his conduct was such that ". . . his confidence in him as a commander was sensibly diminished. The general believed that [Ripley] dreaded *responsibility* more than danger. In short that he had a greater share of physical than moral courage." Brown the man of action was bound to distrust Ripley the man of caution.

Ripley went back to Fort Erie and worked the men night and day building entrenchments and putting guns into position. General Gaines arrived from Sackets Harbor on August 4 and took command. Ripley resumed command of his brigade and, although gloomy and full of doubts, cooperated wholeheartedly with Gaines.

The American preparations for a siege were greatly aided by a mistake by Drummond. If he had attacked Fort Erie immediately, he probably would have won an easy victory. Instead, Drummond waited several days for reinforcements to replace the losses he suffered at Lundy's Lane. That battle had made him cautious and had given him more respect for the American army. He hesitated to attack Gaines and Ripley, although he had 3,150 men to their scant 2,000.

Drummond opened his campaign by sending 600 men across the Niagara River to seize the American supply depot at Black Rock opposite Fort Erie. This force was routed by 240 sharpshooters. Drummond angrily issued an order that blamed the defeat on "the misbehavior of the troops employed."

Not wishing to assault Fort Erie until he had softened its defenses by a bombardment, Drummond sent for heavy siege guns. While he waited for his guns, the Americans were busy on their defenses. They were directed by two engineers who had graduated from West Point, Lieutenant Colonels William McRee and Eleazar D. Wood. When they finished their work, the Americans had a strongly entrenched camp enclosed by 1,500 yards of walls and ditches. (It should be noted here that during the war no fortifications built by West Point graduates were ever taken by the British.) Among the expert artillery commanders defending the fortifications at Erie was Captain Towson, whose guns had done such good work at Chippewa.

Gaines and Ripley and their engineers, McRee and Wood, closely watched the British and concluded that Drummond planned an all-out attack on August 14. The evening of the 13th, Gaines visited every part of Fort Erie defenses. He gave careful directions to the officers and words of encouragement to the troops. Pickets were sent out to prowl the darkness and give warning of an attack. At two o'clock in the morning, the pickets fired and fell back to the fort. They were followed closely by British troops carrying scaling ladders.

The British were divided into three columns: one to assault the left; one, the right; and one, the center of the fortifications. On the left, Towson's guns quickly shot the attacking forces to pieces. In the center, Ripley's troops smashed five separate British assaults. But on the right, a column commanded by Lieutenant Colonel Drummond, nephew of General Drummond, seized the northeast bastion of Fort Erie. (As a major, Drummond had protested Sir George Prevost's hasty retreat from Sackets Harbor.) A savage fighter, Drummond shouted for his men to "give the damned Yankees no quarter!" Vicious hand-to-hand fighting raged in the Fort Erie bastion, and the Americans kept the British from occupying the rest of the fort. But they could not drive Drummond's troops, who were joined by other detachments, out of the bastion. If General Drummond had sent in his reserves at this critical moment, the Americans might have lost Fort Erie. But he did not act.

The Americans hurled several attacks at Colonel Drummond's force, but it hung on. Another attack was being prepared, when, according to a Lieutenant Douglas, "Every sound was hushed by the sense of an unnatural tremor beneath our feet, like the first heave of an earthquake. Almost at the same instant, the center of the bastion burst up with a terrific explosion, and a jet of flame, mingled with fragments of timber, earth, stone and bodies of men, rose to the height of one or two hundred feet in the air, and fell in a shower of ruins to a great distance all around."

Following the explosion, the American artillery opened a heavy fire, and the British broke and fled to their entrenchments. In his report, General Drummond said: "Some ammunition, which had been placed under a platform, caught fire from the firing of guns in the rear, and a most tremendous explosion followed, by which almost all the troops which had entered the place were dreadfully mangled. Panic was instantly communicated to the troops, who could not be persuaded that the explosion was accidental; and the enemy at the same time pressing forward and commencing a heavy fire of musketry, the Fort was abandoned and our troops retreated."

Was the explosion an accident? Historian Benson J. Lossing quotes one of Porter's men as saying: "History ascribes it to accident; and perhaps it would not be proper for me to state what I learned at the time. Even if it was design, I think the end justified the means. It was that mysterious explosion . . . that saved our gallant little army." Lossing then goes on to write: "The venerable Jabez Fisk, now [in 1867] living near Adrian, Michigan, who was in the fight, is not so reticent concerning the explosion. In a letter to me, dated May 20, 1863, he writes: 'Three or four hundred of the enemy had got into the bastion. At this time, an American officer came running up and said, "General Gaines, the bastion is full. I can blow them all to hell in a minute." They both passed back through a stone building, and in a short time the bastion and the British were high in the air.' "

In that battle the Americans lost only 84 men, while the British lost 780 men, killed, wounded, and missing. Of Drummond's column, 188 officers and men out of 190 were reported killed, wounded, or missing. Colonel Drummond was killed, and on his body was found a copy of an order issued by General Drummond. A bayonet had pierced these words in the order: "The Lieut. General most strongly recommends a full use of the bayonet."

Reporting to the secretary of war, Gaines wrote: "It is due to the brave men I have the honor to command that I should say that the affair was to the enemy a sore beating and a defeat; and it was to us a handsome victory." Congress voted Gaines the thanks of the nation and a gold medal. The states of New York, Virginia, and Tennessee each rewarded him with a sword. The cities of Gainesville in Florida, Georgia, and Texas are named in his honor.

In a letter to Governor General Prevost, the frustrated General Drummond blamed the defeat mainly on General L. de Watteville's regiment. This unit, which was composed of German, Polish, and Spanish troops, ran into the sharp-shooting artillery of Captain Towson and fell back after taking heavy losses. Drummond ignored the opposition faced by these troops and said: "The main body of de Watteville's regiment retreated in such confusion that they carried the King's Regiment before them like a torrent. Thus by the misconduct of this foreign corps has the opportunity been totally lost. . . . The agony of mind I suffer from the present disgraceful and unfortunate conduct of the troops committed to my superintendence wounds me to the soul!"

However, the heavy losses suffered by Drummond's troops show clearly that they fought courageously and their conduct was far from "disgraceful." And Drummond never explained why he didn't send his reserve in to support the column that had captured the Fort Erie bastion. Clearly, Drummond sought to cover up his own mistakes by blaming his troops, particularly a "foreign corps." To make good his losses in the Fort Erie assault, Drummond sent to Burlington Heights and York for two more regiments totaling 1,140 men and began a siege of Fort Erie.

In early August, when he could no longer be of service to Brown's army, Chauncey finally took his fleet out on Lake Ontario. He arrived off Fort George on August 5 and then, while Brown's troops were being attacked at Fort Erie, he sailed to blockade Kingston. Chauncey always managed to be in the wrong place at the wrong time. When he heard that Brown's army was besieged at Fort Erie, Chauncey sent a letter, reminding Brown of the harsh message he had written on July 13. "Was it friendly or just or honorable," asked Chauncey, ". . . to infer that I had pledged myself to meet you on a particular day at the head of the Lake, for the purpose of cooperation, and in case of disaster to your army, thus to turn [the public's] resentment from you . . . upon me? . . . You well know, Sir, that the fleet could not have rendered you the least service during your late incursion upon Upper Canada. You have not been able to approach Lake Ontario on any point nearer than Queenston."

The fact remains that when Brown reached Queenston, he was prevented from attacking Fort George because Chauncey's fleet was not on hand with the guns and supplies and troops that were needed. And after the Battle of Lundy's Lane, another fact stood out: British ships had carried reinforcements across Lake Ontario to Riall and Drummond while Chauncey's fleet remained idle in Sackets Harbor.

Still lecturing Brown on how to fight a war, Chauncey wrote: "That you might find the fleet somewhat of a convenience in the transportation of provisions and stores for the use of the army and an agreeable appendage to attend its marching and countermarching, I am ready to believe; but Sir, the Secretary of the Navy has honored me with a high destiny; we intend to seek and fight the enemy's fleet. This is the great purpose of the government in creating this fleet, and I shall not be diverted in my efforts to effectuate it by any sinister attempt to render it subordinate to the army."

In his long-winded discussion, Chauncey ignored the need for army-navy cooperation on the Niagara frontier. Chauncey said "we intend to seek and fight the enemy's fleet," and there was nothing wrong with that. But if Brown had been able, with Chauncey's help, to take Kingston, Yeo's ships would have been "homeless," with no naval base to operate from. They would have had to come out and give Chauncey the fight he said he wanted.

To his credit, Chauncey proved to be a good manager who knew how to direct a shipbuilding program. But he didn't seem to know how to make the best use of his ships against the enemy. He appeared to love his ships so much that he didn't want them to be damaged. An example of this was his gingerly handling of his ships after the "Burlington Races," when he had the British bottled up in Burlington Bay.

After the battle of August 14, the British guns continued to throw shells into Fort Erie but did little damage. Then, on the 20th, a shell exploded in Gaines's quarters and injured him so severely that he had to give up his command and retire to Buffalo. Brown, who was in Batavia, New York, hurried to Fort Erie and issued an order putting Ripley in command. Brown then went to Buffalo and set up headquarters of the Army of the Niagara to keep an eye on Ripley. Several officers soon visited Brown and told him that the army had no confidence in Ripley. They also warned Brown that Ripley still was in favor of abandoning Fort Erie. Although his wound was not healed, Brown decided to go to Fort Erie and take command in person.

13
VICTORY AT PLATTSBURGH

While Drummond's troops were hammering at Fort Erie, the British launched two other attacks that they believed would force the United States to make peace on their terms. The first target was Lake Champlain, long the water highway of armies invading northern New York. Bitter fighting had taken place in this area during the French and Indian War and the Revolution. The other British target was Chesapeake Bay far to the south.

In the summer of 1814, the American land forces at Plattsburgh on Lake Champlain consisted of 6,000 men commanded by Major General George Izard, a well-trained officer and an excellent engineer. When Izard heard that Wellington's veterans were pouring into Canada, he got busy fortifying Plattsburgh. He placed his main defenses on a peninsula formed by the Saranac River and the lake. He built Fort Moreau, named for a French general exiled by Napoleon, plus many blockhouses and batteries of artillery.

The small naval force at Plattsburgh was commanded by Commodore Thomas Macdonough, a 30-year-old veteran of the young navy's war with the Barbary pirates. Macdonough had been at work strengthening his fleet. Noah Brown, a famous shipbuilder from New York City, brought in a work gang to build a corvette. This ship was launched only 40 days after the timbers were cut from nearby forests. Macdonough named her the *Saratoga*. An unfinished ship that had been planned as a steamboat was turned into the schooner *Ticonderoga*. Hearing of British shipbuilding progress in the area, Macdonough appealed to the government for another ship. President Madison himself issued orders, and Noah Brown and his men went to work again. In three and a half weeks, the brig *Eagle* was in the water.

The governor general of Canada, Sir George Prevost, had received orders in June to prepare for an invasion of the United States. The British planned to move down from Lake Champlain to Albany, New York, and cut the New England states off from the rest of the country. An advance south by way of Lake Champlain also would protect an important British supply line. The British army in Canada long had been fed by New York and New England farmers and supply contractors. In a letter to the War Department, General Izard angrily reported this trade with the enemy: "The road to St. Regis is covered with droves of cattle, and the river with rafts, destined for the enemy. . . . On the eastern side of Lake Champlain the high roads are found insufficient for the supplies of cattle which are pouring into Canada. Like herds of buffaloes, they press through the forests, making paths for themselves."

Although it was no secret that the British were massing troops for an attack on Lake Champlain, Secretary of War Armstrong chose to ignore all signs of danger. He issued an incredible order for General Izard to march 4,000 troops westward to Sackets Harbor. From there, Izard was to attack Kingston or aid Brown at Fort Erie. Controlling his temper with difficulty, Izard wrote Armstrong on August 11: "I will make the movement you direct, if possible; but I shall do it with the apprehension of risking the force under my command. . . . [The enemy] is in force superior to mine in my front; he daily threatens an attack on my position at Champlain; we are all in hourly expectation of a serious conflict."

Annoyed that Izard dared question his judgment, Armstrong again ordered Izard to march for Sackets Harbor. "It is very distinctly my opinion," he wrote, "that it has become good policy on our part to carry the war as far to the westward as possible." An amazing opinion, while the British were massing overwhelming forces in the east.

On August 20, Izard again protested to Armstrong: "I must not be responsible for the consequences of abandoning my present strong position." Then, good soldier Izard obeyed orders and started his 130-mile march to Sackets Harbor on August 29. At about the same time, the British crossed the border on their way to Plattsburgh.

Never before had Britain sent to America so powerful an army. Three veteran brigades comprising 10,000 men were commanded by three of Wellington's best generals: Major Generals Frederick P. Robinson, Manley Power, and Thomas Brisbane. Another 4,000 troops were in reserve. However, the one weakness of this army was in its high command. The commander in chief, Sir George Prevost, had proved himself timid and fumbling in the attack on Sackets Harbor, and he was soon quarreling with his brigade commanders, who had no respect for his military abilities.

Facing this powerful British army was a force of only 1,500 regulars and militia commanded by Brigadier General Alexander Macomb, who had won honors during the St. Lawrence expedition. Responding to Macomb's urgent call for volunteers, Major General Benjamin Mooers brought in 700 New York militia. But the stiff-necked, near-sighted governors of the New England states still refused to let their militia serve under the army. The governor of Vermont ordered a brigade of Vermont militia, which had gone to the defense of Plattsburgh, to return home. The Vermonters ignored the governor.

Macomb kept his men busy on the defenses of Plattsburgh. He built two more forts, which he named in honor of Brown and Scott. To gain time, he also sent militia units out to fight a delaying action against the advancing British. The scrappy Major John E. Wool, who had fought brilliantly at Queenston early in the war, led one detachment that proved highly annoying to the enemy. The British finally drove the Americans back to the Saranac River. There, Wool's command was joined by other militia units that helped keep the redcoats from crossing the river.

Prevost reached the Saranac on September 6 and studied Macomb's defenses. He noted that a ridge beyond the river was "crowned with three strong redoubts [Forts Moreau, Scott, and Brown] and other fieldworks and blockhouses armed with heavy ordnance, with their flotilla [Macdonough's fleet] at anchor out of gunshot from the shore." Prevost was a cautious man, but this time he did not exaggerate the strength of the American position. Izard had built a strong defense system, and Macomb had improved it further. He didn't have many trained regulars, but among them were artillerymen who knew how to handle their guns. The news from Chippewa and Lundy's Lane had given Macomb's troops a keen fighting spirit. After losing around 200 men in skirmishing along the Saranac, Prevost went into camp a mile north of Plattsburgh and waited impatiently for the British fleet.

Prevost long had insisted that he could not invade New York unless the British fleet won control of Lake Champlain, his best route for bringing in supplies. So for many days, Prevost had been sending ill-tempered messages to the British naval commander, Captain George Downie. This man was an excellent officer who had served under Nelson when that great admiral beat the French and Spanish fleets at Trafalgar in 1803. When Downie took command on September 2, he found that his most powerful ship, the *Confiance,* was not yet completed. Thus the British fleet had to sail while carpenters were still working on the *Confiance.* Downie was confident, however, that this ship alone could beat the whole American fleet. She carried 37 guns and had a furnace for heating cannon shot, which was a dreaded weapon in the days of wooden ships. Downie's other ships were the *Linnet,* 16 guns, and the *Chub* and *Finch,* each with 11 guns. He also had five gunboats, mounting two guns each, and seven gunboats with one gun each.

Macdonough's fleet consisted of *Saratoga,* 26 guns; *Eagle,* 20 guns; *Ticonderoga,* 17 guns; and *Preble,* 7 guns. In addition, he had six gunboats, each with two guns, and four gunboats with one gun each.

The British fleet carried 90 guns to the American fleet's 86, making them fairly evenly matched. But the British had 60 long-range guns to the Americans' 45. The powerful *Confiance* had 16 long-range guns, while Macdonough's best ship, the *Saratoga,* had only eight. If Downie stayed at long range, he could hammer the American fleet to pieces. Macdonough saw this threat and made plans to meet it. He anchored his four large ships across Plattsburgh Bay, at a point where it was about a mile and a half wide, and placed his gunboats behind them. This position left Downie little room in which to maneuver at long range. He would have to fight at close quarters, within shooting distance of the Americans' heavy short-range guns. The farsighted Macdonough also rigged his ships with anchors and cables so that they could be turned around during the battle. Thus, if the guns on the starboard (right) side of his ships were disabled, he could turn his ships around and bring the guns on the port (left) side into action. Macdonough took one more precaution that was to prove decisive.

He rigged his cables under the water to keep them from being cut by enemy shot during the battle.

A little after eight o'clock on the morning of September 11, Downie's fleet entered Plattsburgh Bay. As the British ships tried to move around the end of the American line, the wind turned cranky—as Macdonough had hoped it would. Unable to maneuver, Downie's ships finally had to anchor within 300 yards of Macdonough's line. *Saratoga*'s first shot, aimed by Macdonough, smashed into *Confiance* and killed a half-dozen men. A shot from *Linnet* demolished a hen coop on *Saratoga* and released a young game-cock, which the seamen, who enjoyed cock fighting, had brought on board. The excited cock jumped on a gun and, flapping its wings, crowed lustily and defiantly. The crew cheered what it considered to be a victory sign.

The cool Downie took punishment from *Saratoga* until he had all the guns on one side of *Confiance* lined up on the American ship. Then a sheet of flame leaped from *Confiance* as she fired a thunderous broadside. The *Saratoga* shook as if she had been hit by a storm. Jagged splinters of wood, as deadly as bullets, flew through the air. One-fifth of the men on Macdonough's ship were killed or wounded, and nearly every man was knocked off his feet. But the American gunners quickly went back to work, and the two ships pounded each other with cannon balls as fast as the guns could be loaded. Macdonough was knocked unconscious twice, but soon was back into action, aiming a gun.

Within the first 15 minutes of battle, the British suffered a severe loss when Captain Downie was killed. But after two hours of slugging, the outcome of the battle hung in the balance. The American ship *Preble* had been disabled, while *Chub* had been lost by the British. Red-hot shot from *Confiance* had twice set *Saratoga* on fire, but Macdonough had put the flames out. Now, every gun on the starboard side of

This map shows the area of operations of General Wilkinson's ill-fated expedition against Montreal. It also shows the Lake Champlain region, where General Macomb and Commodore Macdonough blocked the British advance into New York State.

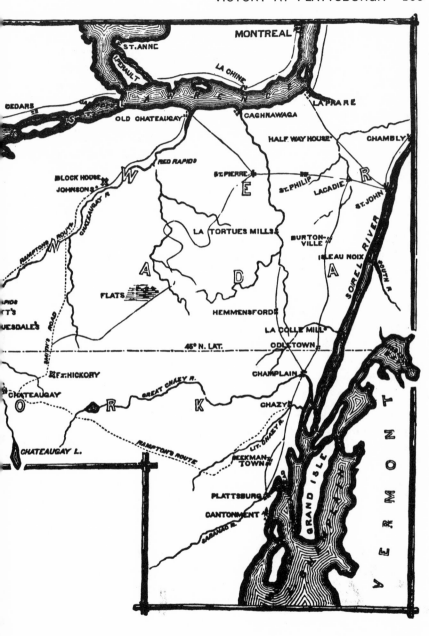

Saratoga had been wrecked, and she was taking a pounding from *Linnet*. Fortunately for Macdonough, most of *Confiance*'s port-side guns had been knocked out, too. At this moment, Macdonough's careful planning saved his ship and won the battle. Hauling on the cables fastened to anchors, the *Saratoga*'s seamen turned their ship around so that her port-side guns could go into action. *Confiance* also tried to turn around, but her anchors had been shot away and she hung helplessly in a half-turn. *Saratoga*'s undamaged guns soon pounded *Confiance* into surrender and then took care of *Linnet,* too. Meanwhile, *Ticonderoga* drove *Finch* aground, and she hauled down her flag. Only the British gunboats, which could use oars, were able to escape. The American ships were so heavily damaged that not a one could hoist a sail and pursue the gunboats.

The Battle of Lake Champlain was one of the most murderous ever fought. "The havoc on both sides was dreadful," wrote Midshipman William Lee of the *Confiance*. "Never was a shower of hail so thick as the shot whistling about our ears. ... There is one of the marines who was in the Trafalgar action with Lord Nelson, who says it was a mere *flea bite* in comparison with this." The British lost 300 killed and wounded out of 937, nearly one out of three. The Americans lost nearly 200 killed and wounded out of 882, about one in four. This battle put an end to British attempts to invade the United States from the north.

Watching from a high point of land, Prevost had ordered his troops to attack when he saw the British fleet go into action. The brigades of Robinson and Power marched to cross the Saranac farther up, while Brisbane's brigade attacked the bridges nearer Plattsburgh. The Robinson-Power column got lost and Brisbane's troops were stalled by stubborn American regulars. Then, cheering from American troops told Prevost that the British fleet had been beaten. He immediately called off the attack. The next morning, after destroying large amounts of supplies and ammunition, the British army began marching back to Canada. Wellington's battle-tested veterans had seen little action.

Prevost was savagely criticized for timidity, even cowardice, by civilians and military men. General Robinson angrily wrote: "I am sick at heart, everything I see and hear is discouraging. . . ."

Prevost insisted that the defeat of the British fleet had made a retreat necessary. If he had gone on and taken Plattsburgh, he would have had to depend on the none-too-good roads to bring in supplies. And as he advanced, his supply line would have been exposed to attack by the American fleet on Lake Champlain. Some military experts, recalling what had happened to Burgoyne in the Revolutionary War, were inclined to agree with Prevost. But the British government ignored his excuses and ordered him to face a court-martial. Prevost died before he could be brought to trial.

14

THE ROCKETS' RED GLARE

The advance of Prevost's army into New York had been aided by attacks on the southern coast of the United States, particularly in the Chesapeake Bay area. During the summer of 1814, the British steadily reinforced the naval units commanded by Admiral Sir Alexander Cochrane, who was based in Bermuda. Then, on July 24, 3,000 troops arrived, commanded by Major General Robert Ross, one of Wellington's most brilliant officers. Admiral Cochrane sailed for Chesapeake Bay on August 1, and was followed on August 4 by another fleet carrying Ross's troops. Reaching the Chesapeake, Admiral Cochrane met Admiral Sir George Cockburn, whose forces had been raiding and burning American coastal towns.

Admiral Cockburn wanted to strike quickly at Washington, D.C., and then march on to Baltimore. Privateers from that city had captured scores of British merchant ships, and Cockburn had threatened to burn out this "nest of pirates." But the cautious Admiral Cochrane first wanted to move up the Patuxent River and destroy a flotilla of American gunboats. This force was commanded by Commodore Joshua Barney, who had fought in 17 naval actions during the Revolutionary War. Barney's gunboats had been giving Admiral Cockburn a busy time. In June, the British went up the Patuxent twice to get the American gunboats, but were driven back with heavy losses. So Admiral Cockburn blockaded the mouth of the Patuxent with several ships and waited for Admiral Cochrane to arrive.

When General Ross's troops joined the forces of Cochrane and Cockburn based at Benedict, Maryland, the British had a total of 4,000 men, infantry, sailors, and marines. It seemed risky for them to march inland with this small expedition. But they were aided greatly by the muddled state of American defenses. President Madison had tried for several months to strengthen the defenses of Washington, while most of his cabinet members doubted the danger. Secretary of War Armstrong, who was busy masterminding the actions of General Izard at Plattsburgh, scoffed at the idea that the British might attack Washington. Despite opposition, on July 2 the President finally got the cabinet to establish a new military district for the defense of the nation's capital. It was, however, put under the command of Brigadier General William Winder, almost guaranteeing that nothing good would come of this move. Winder had been captured during the disgraceful defeat at Stoney Creek and had been exchanged by the British in the spring of 1814. But Winder's uncle, Lavin Winder, was the Federalist governor of Maryland, and President Madison hoped that the nephew's appointment would gain the national government Federalist party support in that state.

Winder wore himself out rushing about the countryside, scouting and inspecting defenses (but building none) and calling for volunteers. He had less than 1,000 trained regulars and a few thousand raw militia. Armstrong, who disliked Winder, did little to cooperate with him. Still convinced of his military genius, Armstrong issued a blizzard of orders that added to the confusion. President Madison finally asked him to stop.

On August 18, Ross's infantry started marching up the Patuxent River while Admiral Cockburn's marines and sailors pushed up the river in 40 boats. As the British approached, Commodore Barney, on orders from Secretary of the Navy Jones, destroyed his flotilla. Although the British were marching through a wooded country on narrow roads, General Winder made no effort to delay their advance by having the militia fell trees across roads or snipe at the British from ambush.

When the British reached Bladensburg, five miles from Washington, they faced an American army of around 7,000 men, mostly militia. President Madison was on hand to observe while Secretary of War Armstrong kept insisting that he should be given command. Secretary of State James Monroe and General Winder both bustled about, moving troops here and there. The American force wound up in three lines, none of which could support the others when the British attacked. One of the few professionals on the field was Commodore Barney, whose 500 tough sailors and marines manned five heavy naval guns.

Ross's troops attacked, and the American lines soon dissolved in a panic known as the "Bladensburg Races." But Barney's men stood their ground and shot up one of Ross's regiments. Fnally, Ross outflanked the Americans and forced them to retreat. Barney, who was wounded and captured, was treated with great kindness by Ross.

British troops marched into Washington at eight o'clock in the evening of August 24. President and Mrs. Madison joined hundreds of officials, congressmen, clerks, and citizens in fleeing to the countryside. That night, the invaders burned the Capitol, the President's House, the Treasury, the War Office, and the office of the *National Intelligencer*. Admiral Cockburn took particular pleasure in helping burn this newspaper's office because it had bitterly criticized his raids along the coast.

During the evening, a tornado swept the city, and the next day, an explosion of a powder magazine killed and injured almost 100 of Ross's troops. The British answered criticism of their destruction of public property in Washington by saying this was in retaliation for the ravaging of the Niagara village of Newark and the burning of government buildings in York. The British government also believed that the Washington raid would make the Americans more eager to seek peace on any terms. Instead, after the gloom that follows defeat had dissipated, an angry determination to support the war swept the nation. Many Federalists, who had wanted nothing to do with "Mr. Madison's war," began joining the army. By September 1814, the army totaled 35,000 men, as originally planned in January 1812.

The British army left Washington on August 25 and returned to their base at Benedict on the 30th. While Ross's troops rested, Baltimore prepared for an attack. Militia swarmed into the city and were efficiently organized by Major General Samuel Smith, a United States senator and militia officer. Smith was a tough old Revolutionary War veteran who knew how to lead men. He used loud talk and political pull to keep General Winder from taking command of the troops in Baltimore.

Summing up Winder's career, Henry Adams wrote: "When he might have prepared defenses, he acted as a scout; when he might have fought, he still scouted; when he retreated, he retreated in the wrong direction; when he fought, he thought only of retreat; and whether scouting, retreating or fighting, he never [had] an idea."

In Baltimore at the time were three brilliant naval officers, Commodores John Rodgers, David Porter, and Oliver Hazard Perry. The British blockade had kept these officers from taking their ships to sea, so they put their sailors to work building fortifications.

After their return to Washington, senators and representatives met in the Post Office. People on the streets denounced and threatened Secretary Armstrong, and President Madison hinted strongly that he should resign. Armstrong quit on September 4, and James Monroe took charge of both the War and State departments.

Unlike Winder, who did nothing to slow the British advance on Washington, General Smith sent out strong forces of militia to harass the enemy. General Ross landed his troops near Baltimore on September 12 and soon ran into strong opposition. Riding at the head of a column, General Ross was killed and Colonel Arthur Brooke took command. But the fighting spirit of the redcoats was dulled by the death of their popular general. On September 13, Admiral Cochrane's fleet anchored near Fort McHenry and began a bombardment, and Colonel Brooke's force attacked the American entrenchments. A 25-hour bombardment made no impression on Fort McHenry, and Brooke ran into stiff resistance from General Smith's militia. Cochrane and Brooke talked things over and decided that the taking of Baltimore would prove too costly. The British force sailed away on September 14.

Francis Scott Key, a Washington lawyer, watched the attack on Fort McHenry while aboard a British vessel. He had gone out to the fleet to arrange for the release of an American prisoner. The American flag was still there at dawn, and Key was inspired to scribble some verses that became the national anthem, *The Star-Spangled Banner.*

Victory at Baltimore and on Lake Champlain was soon followed by startling news from Fort Erie, where General Brown had not been idle.

15

BROWN'S MASTER STROKE

On September 2, General Brown returned to Fort Erie and took command from General Ripley. Brown noted that the British had advanced their entrenchments to within 500 yards of the American defenses. They also were completing work on a third battery of heavy guns that could pour a deadly fire into the fort. And since General Drummond's army outnumbered Brown's by about two to one, the threat of a sudden, overwhelming bombardment and assault increased daily.

Brown studied the problem and decided to attack first in order to throw Drummond off balance. He observed the British lines carefully and questioned British deserters. Brown noted that Drummond's army was divided into three brigades, which took turns on duty in the entrenchments. Deserters told him that Drummond's troops, which were camped on low, marshy ground, were weakened by typhoid fever. So Brown planned a sortie "to storm the batteries, destroy the cannon and roughly handle the brigade on duty before those in reserve could be brought into action."

Brown discussed his plan with a council of officers on

September 9, but got little encouragement from most of them. They said that the British lines were not only strong but were defended by some of the best troops in the army, including Scots Highlanders. Brown stamped angrily from the meeting and told General Peter Porter to send out a call for more volunteers.

Major Jesup, who visited Brown a few days later, wrote that the general "was evidently much disappointed at the results of the council. In the course of the evening, he expressed himself with great warmth in regard to his disappointment and in relation to some of the officers who had been present. . . . But [Brown] added, in a manner peculiarly emphatic, 'We must keep our own counsels; the impression must be made that we are done with the affairs, but, as sure as there is a God in heaven, the enemy shall be attacked in his works and beaten, too, as soon as all the volunteers shall have [arrived].' " From that time, added Jesup, "the major general acted and spoke as though he relied for safety on the defense of his camp." Brown also sent spies as deserters into the British lines to say that the Americans were not planning an attack, and were content to let the British make the next move.

When General Porter reported that 1,000 volunteers had arrived, Brown got ready for action. On September 17, he told Ripley, his second in command, and his engineer officers, Colonels McRee and Wood, that he planned to attack that day. As usual, Ripley objected. During the British attack on Fort Erie in August, Ripley had shown great courage, but talk of an attack seemed always to fill him with doubts and fears. According to Brown, "General Ripley contented himself with saying that the enterprise was a hopeless one, and he should be well satisfied to escape from the disgrace which, in his judgment, would fall upon all engaged in it."

Brown's attacking force was divided into three columns. One, under General Porter, was composed of three detachments led by Colonel James Gibson, Colonel Wood of the engineers, and Brigadier General Daniel Davis of the New York militia. The second column, consisting of remnants of the 9th, 11th, and 19th Regiments, was commanded by Colonel James Miller, the hero of Lundy's Lane. The third column, which was held in reserve, consisted of the 21st Regiment and was commanded by General Ripley.

Drummond's reports to his superiors indicated that he expected to be attacked and welcomed a chance to deal out punishment to the Americans. But for a commander who expected action, Drummond was exceedingly careless. He neglected to send out patrols in front of his lines, and American engineers were not spotted as they cut paths to within a few hundred feet of the British entrenchments.

At three o'clock in the afternoon of September 17, General Porter's column, under cover of a heavy rain and thick fog, swarmed over battery No. 3 and also captured the blockhouse in the rear. Cannon were destroyed and the ammunition magazine blown up as untrained militia charged and broke lines held by tough Scots Highlanders. At the same time, Colonel Miller's column captured battery No. 2 and its blockhouse. An attack was then launched on battery No. 1. By this time, heavy British reinforcements had arrived and battery No. 1 could not be taken. Before the Americans finally fell back to their lines, Brown had ordered General Ripley's reserve to the aid of Porter and Miller. The three commanders of Porter's column—Davis, Gibson, and Wood —were killed and Porter and Ripley were wounded. Although Brown was still crippled by his severe hip wound, he was in the front lines with his troops.

The Americans lost 511 men killed, wounded, and missing, while the British loss was even more severe—609 killed, wounded, and missing, plus 385 prisoners. In his report to the secretary of war, Brown wrote: "Thus one thousand regulars, and an equal portion of militia, in one hour of close action, blasted the hopes of the enemy, destroyed the fruits of fifty days labor, and diminished his effective force by one thousand men at least."

Brown's victory, following so soon after the successes on Lake Champlain and at Baltimore, did much to sweep away the gloom that had spread over the nation because of the British capture of Washington. Congress voted the thanks of the nation and gold medals to Brown, Porter, Miller, and Ripley. Major Jesup wrote: "The sortie from Fort Erie was by far the most splendid achievement of the campaign, whether we consider the boldness of the conception, the excellence of the plan, or the ability of the execution. No event in military history, on the same scale, has ever surpassed it. The whole credit is due to General Brown. The writer was in a situation to know that the conception, plan and execution were all his own."

British historian Sir William F. Napier agreed with Jesup. He wrote that Brown's attack was "the only instance in history where a besieging army was entirely broken up and routed by a single sortie."

Henry Adams contended that "among all the American major generals, Brown alone made raw troops as steady as grenadiers and caused militia to storm entrenched lines held by British regulars."

On the other hand, General Drummond contended that his troops had beaten an American force of "not less than five thousand men, including militia." But at the same time, he realized that he could not continue to besiege Fort Erie. Three of his heavy bombardment guns had been wrecked by Brown's troops, and his losses by sickness as well as battle were growing heavier each day. On September 21, Drummond wrote Prevost: "Within the last few days, the sickness of the troops has increased to such an alarming degree . . . that I feel it my duty no longer to persevere in a vain attempt to maintain the blockade of so vastly superior and increasing a force of the enemy under the circumstances. I have therefore given orders for the troops to fall back toward the Chippewa, and shall commence my movement at eight o'clock this evening."

Never admitting that he might possibly be at fault for his setbacks, Drummond continued to claim that he either was outnumbered or his troops did not behave properly in action.

General Izard's army of 4,000 men, which had been sent off on a wild-goose chase by Armstrong, arrived at Sackets Harbor on September 17. There, Izard received no orders from the government, but did get a message from Brown, dated September 10, asking for reinforcements. Violent storms delayed the movement of Izard's troops, and he did not reach Fort Erie until September 27. By this time, Brown had forced Drummond to retreat, and Macdonough and Macomb had beaten Prevost at Plattsburgh. During all this time, Izard's men had done nothing but march several hundred miles.

As Brown's superior officer, Izard took command of the army on the Niagara frontier. The restless, combative Brown did not get along well with the cautious Izard, a well-educated officer who had read all the books on military affairs but lacked Brown's drive and fighting spirit. The impatient Brown pointed out that Drummond's army, reduced by disease and battle losses to 2,500 men, was within easy reach at Chippewa. With the addition of Izard's 4,000, the American army numbered 5,500 regulars and 800 militia, and more volunteers were coming in daily. Before winter put a stop to the fighting, there was time for Izard's army to attack and destroy Drummond's forces and push on into Canada. Finally, Izard agreed to advance.

On October 13, the army marched, and then suddenly stopped. Three days later, Izard wrote to the secretary of war: "I have just learned that Commodore Chauncey with the whole of his fleet has retired into port, and is throwing up batteries for its protection. This defeats all the objects of the operations by land in this quarter. I may [advance to] Chippewa, and should General Drummond not retire, may succeed in giving him a good deal of trouble; but if he falls back on Fort George or Burlington Heights, every step I take in pursuit exposes me to be cut off by the large reinforcements it is in the power of the enemy to throw upon my flank and rear."

Izard's was the largest American army ever assembled on the Niagara frontier. But his fears of the unknown—of what the enemy might do—stalled him in his tracks. In much worse circumstances, Brown had fought at Chippewa, Lundy's Lane, and at Fort Erie. Izard, however, seemed not to remember the right pages in all the military books he had studied. After a few skirmishes with Drummond's army, Izard ordered his troops to fall back to Fort Erie. The army's only accomplishment was the capture of 200 bushels of wheat.

Losing confidence in Izard, the government ordered him to call off the campaign and get out of Canada. The disgusted Brown, at his own request, was sent with a division to Sackets Harbor, where the jittery Chauncey was expecting an attack. The rest of the army was put into winter quarters at Buffalo. Fort Erie was blown up on November 5, and all fighting ended on the Niagara frontier.

Disturbed by his failure, Izard was still generous in his attitude toward Brown. Recognizing Brown's ability to lead militia, Izard wrote the secretary of war: "General Brown is certainly a brave, intelligent, and active officer. Where a portion of the forces is composed of irregular troops (militia),

I have no hesitation in acknowledging my conviction of his being better qualified than I to make them useful in the public service."

On December 18, Izard offered his resignation to the secretary of war in a message that clearly showed his lack of confidence: "I am fully aware that attempts have been made to lessen the confidence of government as well as the public in my ability to execute the important duties intrusted to me—duties which were imposed unexpectedly and much against my inclination. It is therefore not improbable that my voluntary retirement will relieve the Department of War from some embarrassment. . . ."

Secretary of War Monroe did not accept Izard's resignation, but the general's military career was ruined.

16
THE HARTFORD CONVENTION

Throughout the summer and fall of 1814, the British navy had been busy raiding the New England coast from Maine to Connecticut. Eastport and Castine in the District of Maine were occupied, and the Passamaquoddy and Penobscot areas were declared a British possession. (Maine was then governed as a part of Massachusetts. It became a separate state in 1820.) After ignoring "Mr. Madison's war" and refusing to send militia to fight with the army, Federalist party leaders in Massachusetts were jolted into action. Governor Caleb Strong persuaded the legislature to approve the recruiting of 10,000 militia and a loan of one million dollars. The governor then tried to get the War Department to pay for the upkeep of the militia. Since Massachusetts still had no intention of placing its militia under army control, the War Department, now headed by James Monroe, said no.

The legislature angrily declared that since the government wasn't protecting the state, it would refuse to pay any more taxes to the government in Washington. Late in October, the legislature called for a convention of New England states to meet on December 15 and discuss "public grievances and concerns." A strong minority of Republicans objected to this action, but the legislature ignored all protests and appointed 12 delegates to represent Massachusetts. Connecticut accepted the invitation, and the legislature appointed eight delegates. Rhode Island also accepted, but Vermont's legislature refused to appoint delegates and New Hampshire did not reply. Some Federalist orators and many newspapers boldly proposed that the New England states secede from the Union and establish an independent republic.

When the delegates met in Hartford, Connecticut, men of good sense quickly won control of the convention. George Cabot of Massachusetts, who was elected chairman, bluntly said: "We are going to keep you young hotheads from getting into mischief." And the Hartford Convention's final report proved to be rather mild. Mainly, the New Englanders proposed amendments to the Constitution that would weaken the influence of the South in the government in Washington. One amendment proposed to base representation in the House on the number of free persons in a state, thereby reducing the number of Southerners in the House. (Slaves were counted as three-fifths of a person in the Constitution.) Another amendment would have limited a president to one term in office and prohibited a state from having two presidents in succession. This amendment was aimed at Virginia, which had held the presidency for 22 out of 26 years.

Seemingly having learned nothing from the failure of the militia (except when led by Brown or Jackson), the New England delegates insisted that the states should set up their own defenses, paid for out of national taxes.

Massachusetts appointed three and Connecticut two "ambassadors" to deliver the convention's complaints and proposals to Congress. While on their way to Washington, the "ambassadors" ran into parades celebrating Andrew Jackson's startling victory at New Orleans. When they got to Washington, they heard that the war was over—a treaty of peace had been signed at Ghent, Belgium. The embarrassed "ambassadors" left their recommendations with a committee of the House and quickly left town.

17
THE TREATY OF GHENT

Peace talks seeking to end the war had started soon after it began. But they quickly collapsed when the United States insisted that Britain cease her practice of impressment. Tsar Alexander I of Russia then offered to mediate the dispute between the United States and Britain. Early in 1813 the war was going badly for the Americans, and President Madison was anxious to talk peace. He appointed Albert Gallatin, his secretary of the treasury, and James Bayard, a Federalist, as peace commissioners to join John Quincy Adams, who had been appointed the U.S. minister in Russia after resigning from the Senate. They sat around for months while the Tsar was busy with military affairs. Then, in January 1814, Britain politely but firmly refused the Tsar's offer to mediate. The British government said, however, that it would be willing to talk peace directly with American commissioners. Madison immediately added Henry Clay and Jonathan Russell to the American peace delegation. He reminded them that no peace treaty could be signed that did not call for an end to Britain's impressment policy.

Gallatin and Bayard left Russia and went to Britain in an effort to speed up peace talks. They found Britain, celebrating the victory over Napoleon, in no mood to hurry up peace negotiations. The newspapers were full of demands that the United States be punished. Opposing this spirit of revenge, one English paper, *Cobbett's Weekly Register,* declared: "Such men, if men we ought to call such monsters, talk with delight of sending Wellington's army to the U.S.; they revel at the idea of burning the cities and towns, the mills and manufactories of that country."

Gallatin sampled British public opinion, found it grim, and wrote President Madison that the impressment issue should not be dragged into the peace talks. On June 27, 1814, a gloomy meeting of Madison and his cabinet studied Gallatin's warning as well as the sad state of affairs in the nation. The treasury was practically empty, British naval forces were running wild along the East Coast, and the American army soon would have to face Wellington's veterans. The President and his cabinet decided to seek peace and forget about impressment. These instructions reached the American peace commissioners as they prepared to open negotiations with the British at Ghent, Belgium, on August 8, 1814.

The British peace commission was headed by Admiral Lord Gambier, who had commanded the fleet that bombarded Copenhagen in 1807. The other commissioners were Henry Goulburn, the young, violently anti-American undersecretary of war, and William Adams, a little-known doctor of civil law. Britain certainly had not sent its "first team" to negotiate with the Americans. None of the British were as capable as the American commissioners. It soon became clear that the British commissioners could scarcely clear their throats without checking first with Lord Castlereagh, the foreign minister.

Confident that the military news from Prevost at Plattsburgh would be good, Castlereagh had his commissioners present harsh peace terms. They demanded the creation of an Indian state consisting of almost everything north of the Ohio River and sweeping far west. This state would form a permanent barrier between American and Canadian western settlements. The Great Lakes were to be taken wholly within Canada, and the Canadian boundary would run from Lake Superior to the Mississippi River north of the Ohio. This would give Britain the right to navigate that waterway. Finally, enough of Maine was to be surrendered to provide a land route from Halifax to Quebec. Adams was jolted by these demands, but he coolly asked the British to write them down for careful consideration. Then, he and the other commissioners worked all night to write a brilliant refusal and immediately prepared to leave Ghent. Not wanting the peace talks to collapse, Castlereagh instructed the British commissioners to drop the demand for an Indian state. Still sure of the success of British forces in America, Castlereagh proposed a treaty based on *status uti possidetis*—that is, the state of possession at the conclusion of the fighting. (In other words, each side would keep the territory it won during the war.) The American commissioners rejected this and called for *status quo ante bellum*—or the condition existing before the war. (No territory would change hands.)

The peace talks were deadlocked when, toward the end of October, news came of Prevost's retreat into Canada, the repulse at Baltimore, the death of Ross, and Drummond's hasty retreat from Fort Erie. The British government faced the choice of making a peace that gave it no territorial gains or of sending more troops to Canada. Continuing the war would mean that taxes would remain high, and the British people were already loudly demanding that they be cut. Furthermore, it might be risky to send more troops to Canada while affairs in Europe were far from quiet. Britain's allies—

Prussia, Austria, and Russia—had been united in defeating Napoleon, but now they were quarreling over the peace settlement. Russia's growing influence in western Europe was particularly disturbing to the British. On November 4, the government turned for advice to the Duke of Wellington. He was asked to take over the command in Canada, with full powers "to make peace, or to continue the war with renewed vigor."

The Duke studied the maps and Prevost's reports and replied: "That which appears to me to be wanting in America is not a general, or general officers and troops, but a naval superiority on the Lakes. The question is, whether we can acquire this. If we can't, I shall do you but little good in America, and I shall go there only to prove the truth of Prevost's defense; and to sign a peace which might as well be signed now."

The Duke had hit upon the weak point in any new campaign. For the second time in a year, and the second time in history, a British fleet had been forced to surrender. Control of the Great Lakes clearly appeared to be beyond the power of the British in Canada. Coming back to the peace talks, the blunt Duke wrote: "In regard to your negotiation, I confess that I think you have no right, from the state of the war, to demand any concession of territory. . . . You can get no territory; indeed, the state of your military operations however creditable does not entitle you to any."

Wellington's advice to make peace was supported by two British officers who had fought at Lundy's Lane. General Phineas Riall, who had been captured and had lost an arm, and Major John M. Wilson, who had been wounded seven times, told the government what to expect if it again challenged an army commanded by General Brown. Although Brown's Niagara campaign had won no territory, he and Scott had made their presences felt at London and in Ghent.

If the British officials needed any more convincing, American privateers helped them make up their minds. In the final months of the war, the British lost an average of two merchant ships a day. One ship out of every 10 that sailed from a British port was captured. Insurance rates soared to three times what they had been during the height of the war with Napoleon. The *Chasseur,* out of Baltimore and commanded by Captain Thomas Boyle, captured more than 30 ships, many of them in the English Channel. Boyle sent the insurance men at Lloyd's of London into a rage by jokingly proclaiming that "the United Kingdom of Great Britain and Ireland [are] in a state of strict and vigorous blockade." The Royal Navy sent out several warships to hunt down the *Chasseur.* To her misfortune, one British warship, the brig *St. Lawrence,* found the American privateer and *Chasseur* captured her after a 20-minute fight.

Earlier, *Leo* of Baltimore had made the Duke of Wellington painfully aware of American sea power. She had captured a British ship carrying the Duke's paymaster and uniforms for his army in Spain.

Another Baltimore privateer, *Harpy,* loitered for weeks between Liverpool and Dublin, cutting off mail service between England and Ireland. British authorities even advised merchants that it was unsafe to send ships from Bristol to Plymouth without protection. The prices of such delicacies as sugar and coffee jumped 200 percent. The harried merchants of Glasgow, Scotland, finally sent a complaint to the government: "When we have declared the whole American coast under blockade, it is equally distressing and mortifying that our ships cannot with safety traverse our own channels." During the war, a total of 1,700 British merchant ships valued at more than $40 million were taken by 500 American privateers. The small American navy of only 22 ships captured 165 British vessels.

Probably the most efficient and deadly of the U.S. Navy's light warships was the sloop-of-war *Wasp*. She was commanded by Master Commandant Johnston Blakely, a fiery North Carolinian. *Wasp* was the second sloop of war to bear that name. (The first *Wasp* had been captured by the British.) Late in the spring of 1814, Blakely deftly maneuvered his ship through the British blockade, and within a few weeks had captured five British merchant vessels. Soon *Wasp* was prowling the English Channel, where she tangled with the British warship *Reindeer*. The British vessel was captured after a sharp fight that cost her 67 killed and wounded out of a crew of 118. *Wasp* lost only 5 killed and 22 wounded. After repairing minor damage to his ship, Blakely took three more British ships.

On September 1, Blakely spotted a convoy of 10 vessels guarded by the British battleship *Armada,* carrying 74 guns. *Armada* took after *Wasp,* which easily outran the big battleship and circled back to attack the convoy. While *Armada* was trying to catch up, *Wasp* captured and burned a ship carrying valuable military stores. But the captain of *Armada* could do nothing but rant and swear.

Later, *Wasp* got into a night battle with the British brig *Avon.* In spite of the darkness, *Wasp*'s gunners shot *Avon* to pieces, and the Americans were preparing to board the British brig when two more enemy brigs approached. Both of them went to the aid of the sinking *Avon* and let *Wasp* alone. On October 9, *Wasp* met a Swedish brig and took from her two American officers who had been captured on *Essex* but had escaped from the British. After that, nothing more was ever heard of *Wasp.* She simply disappeared without a trace in the vast Atlantic Ocean.

Wasp was no more, but she had proved to the British that they would have to protect their merchant-vessel convoys with greater numbers of fighting ships. This, in turn, would leave a good many other ships unprotected and easy pickings for American privateers. And soon *Chasseur, Harpy,* and dozens of other privateers went to work with painful results for British merchants and the embarrassed Royal Navy.

Adding up all the bad news from land and sea, the British government instructed its commissioners to seek a peace without territorial gains. And the American commissioners made no mention of the issue of impressment. The treaty that was signed at Ghent on December 24, 1814, restored the *status quo ante bellum.* No territory was to change hands. The questions involving fishing rights and the U.S.-Canadian border were to be settled by commissioners from the two nations. If they could not agree, a third nation would be called on to work out settlements.

The *Times* of London was not happy with the Treaty of Ghent. It said: "The war—to speak tenderly of it—has not been a very glorious one." The newspaper went on to regret "that the war had closed without wiping off our naval and military disgraces." Calling the Americans "vain, boastful and insolent," the *Times* thought Britain should "grapple with the young lion" now, rather than wait till it was even stronger.

In the United States, the Federalists sneered because no mention of impressment was made in the treaty. But never again did a British ship stop an American vessel and impress a seaman. The United States had won the rights accorded an independent nation by being willing to fight for them.

Before the Treaty of Ghent was ratified by the British and Americans, a final campaign was fought to a bloody finish in the South.

18

VICTORY AT NEW ORLEANS

While the American and British peace commissioners were arguing at Ghent in August 1814, the British government was making plans for an expedition against New Orleans. Control of that port would deprive the Mississippi Valley states of a vital gateway to the sea. With the mouth of the Mississippi River in their hands, the British would have a strong bargaining weapon to use against the Americans.

Their plans called for Admiral Cochrane's fleet to take General Ross's 3,000 troops to Jamaica, where they would be joined by several thousand more troops from England. Ross was to command the expedition. But when Ross's death in Baltimore was reported, Major General Sir Edward Pakenham, a popular, courageous officer and brother-in-law of the Duke of Wellington, was put in command. The expedition was ordered to sail from Jamaica by November 22. Pakenham had not arrived by then, so the fleet sailed without him. The acting commander of the troops was Major General John Keane, who looked to Admiral Cochrane for advice since the admiral was older and more experienced.

Admiral Cochrane had big plans to rally hordes of Indians to aid the expedition against New Orleans. He ignored the fact that Major General Andrew Jackson's crushing defeat of the Creeks at the Battle of Horseshoe Bend on March 27, 1814, had shattered Indian power in the South. The failure of a British force to take Fort Bowyer at Mobile on September 15 also blocked British efforts to recruit Indian allies. Then, early in November, Jackson had attacked and destroyed the defenses at Pensacola, in Spanish Florida, which the British had been using as a base to supply Indians in the area.

On December 8, Admiral Cochrane's fleet moved into the entrance of Lake Borgne, a wide, shallow inlet in the Gulf of Mexico whose western and northern shores were within a few miles of New Orleans. American gunboats on the lake were sunk after a sharp battle. Then, barges rowed by sailors carried General Keane's troops across the lake. Pushing up an unguarded bayou and routing a militia outfit, the British finally reached Villeré plantation, only nine miles from New Orleans, on December 23. Meanwhile, General Jackson was shaking up the drowsy city by placing it under military rule and calling for volunteers. If Keane had pushed on immediately from Villeré plantation, he could have taken New Orleans. But prisoners told him wild stories about 12,000 troops being in the city. Keane decided to wait for reinforcements and the arrival of the commander in chief, General Pakenham.

General Jackson wasted no time. He collected a force of 2,000 men, composed of U.S. army regulars, Tennessee, Louisiana, and Mississippi militiamen, plus 200 free Negroes, and immediately attacked the British. On the night of December 23, Jackson's men smashed into Keane's camp and fought a hand-to-hand battle for four hours. The British regulars held their ground, but they lost more heavily than the Americans:

46 killed, 167 wounded, and 64 missing; to 24 killed, 115 wounded, and 74 missing.

On December 24, Jackson pulled his troops back two miles to the Rodriguez Canal, which stretched over one thousand yards from the Mississippi River to a cypress swamp. The canal was about 10 feet wide and three to five feet deep. Jackson had already put men to work building embankments of earth, logs, and cotton bales behind the canal. Twenty heavy guns were put in the line, several of them manned by Jean Lafitte's pirates. The right and center of the line were defended by New Orleans, Louisiana, and Mississippi militia and two regular army regiments. On the left were 2,000 sharpshooting Tennessee riflemen commanded by Generals William Carroll and John Coffee. Ironically, while Jackson's troops prepared for battle, American representatives in Ghent were signing the treaty of peace.

The handsome, dashing General Pakenham arrived on Christmas Day and cheered up his half-frozen, mud-covered troops. He soon put them to work dragging heavy guns to bombard the American defenses. Their back-breaking labor accomplished nothing because the American guns, particularly those handled by Lafitte's pirates, proved more accurate than the British, and Pakenham had to call off the bombardment. He then decided to wait for reinforcements under Major General John Lambert.

Pakenham was needled by gruff, blustering Admiral Cochrane, who said that 1,000 of his sailors could beat Jackson's rabble. General Lambert's troops arrived early in January, and Pakenham made plans for an assault on January 8, 1815. Three columns of troops under Generals Keane, Lambert, and Gibbs would attack the main American position. Another column, commanded by Colonel William Thornton, would cross the Mississippi and attack the Americans on the west bank.

At six o'clock on the foggy morning of January 8, the British and American guns opened fire and long lines of red-coats moved slowly, in perfect step, into the fog and smoke. Artillery tore holes in the British lines and twice they were halted, re-formed, and again advanced. Although the British were punished by artillery, it was Jackson's riflemen who really slaughtered them. Rifle fire flickered and flamed continuously from the muddy, brown embankment, and hundreds of British soldiers fell.

General Gibbs was mortally wounded and his troops began to retreat. When General Pakenham rode up to rally the men, he, too, was mortally wounded. General Keane now took command and led the 93rd Highlanders to aid Gibbs's troops. He was wounded, and the 93rd, which went into action with 925 men, lost 800 killed and wounded. General Lambert, who suddenly found himself in command of the army, wisely called off the attack. Across the river, Colonel Thornton's column had captured several guns, but it was a wasted victory. In 45 minutes, the British had lost more than 2,000 men killed and wounded and 500 prisoners. The Americans had lost seven men killed and six wounded along the canal embankment. On the night of January 18, the British finally withdrew to their ships.

News of Jackson's victory reached Washington on February 4. Ten days later, the treaty of peace arrived from Ghent. It had been signed two weeks before the Battle of New Orleans, but it still had not been ratified by both governments.

The question arises: if the British had won at New Orleans would they have been able to hold on to the city? This question still stirs historians. Napoleon's escape from Elba in February 1815 plunged Britain back into a fight to the finish with France, and might have forced the British to withdraw their troops from New Orleans. Then, too, Britain would have faced serious problems on the northern frontier. Before news of the signing of the peace treaty had arrived, General Brown was in Washington discussing a spring campaign. He proposed to march against Montreal with an army of 20,000 regulars and 30,000 New York and Vermont militia. British veterans of Chippewa and Lundy's Lane had already told their government what to expect if it challenged Brown.

Whatever the historical "ifs," Andrew Jackson's sharpshooters settled the question by smashing one of the strongest invasion forces ever assembled by Britain. And Jackson's victory pointed him down the political road that was in time to lead him to the presidency.

A British official, carrying the government's ratification of the treaty, arrived in New York on February 11. Hearing of Jackson's victory, he hurried to Washington and presented the ratification to President Madison. The President sent the treaty to the Senate, which ratified it on February 16. The next day, President Madison proclaimed that the war was over.

19

THE NAVY HAS THE LAST WORD

For several months after the Treaty of Ghent had been ratified, American warships, not knowing this news, were busy doing what came naturally—capturing British warships and merchant vessels. On December 17, 1814, a few days before the peace treaty was signed, the frigate *Constitution* slipped through the British blockade and went looking for trouble. "Old Ironsides" was commanded by Captain Charles Stewart. He was one of the officers who, in the summer of 1812, had persuaded President Madison to let American warships go out and fight the enemy despite the British blockade.

Then, in mid-January, a month before news of Ghent arrived, Commodore Stephen Decatur's squadron wriggled out of New York Harbor during a storm that had scattered the British blockade. Decatur's squadron consisted of the frigate *President* (Decatur commanding) and two fighting "cousins" of *Wasp,* the sloop-of-war *Hornet,* commanded by Captain James Biddle, and *Peacock* (named for a British sloop captured by *Hornet* in February 1813), commanded by Captain Lewis Warrington. Decatur's warships were ordered to seek and destroy British merchant vessels in the Indian Ocean.

Unfortunately, Decatur's pilot blundered and the *President* grounded on Sandy Hook in Lower New York Harbor. Her hull and masts were damaged and a heavy wind prevented Decatur from taking her back into the harbor. So he sailed southeast, and the next day found himself in the middle of the British blockading fleet. The crippled *President* could not evade her pursuers, and after a fight in which a fifth of her crew was killed and wounded, the American frigate surrendered.

Knowing nothing of the *President*'s misfortune, *Hornet* and *Peacock* and a supply ship, *Tom Bowline,* sailed for the island of Tristan da Cunha in the South Atlantic Ocean where they were to meet Decatur. During this voyage, *Hornet* separated from *Peacock* to chase and capture a British merchant vessel. Shortly after that, Captain Biddle's ship tangled with the British sloop-of-war *Penguin*. In 22 minutes, *Hornet* pounded *Penguin* into submission, killing and wounding 41 men out of a crew of 122. The American ship lost only two killed and nine wounded. Two days later *Hornet* was joined by *Peacock* and *Tom Bowline*. Prisoners of war were put on *Bowline* and she sailed for Rio de Janeiro, Brazil. After waiting in vain for Decatur, Biddle and Warrington decided to go on alone to the Indian Ocean.

On April 27, *Hornet* again pulled away from *Peacock* to chase a vessel, which turned out to be the British line-of-battleship *Cornwallis,* with 74 guns. Soon, *Cornwallis* was chasing *Hornet,* and the British warship proved to be very fast for so big a vessel. Her gunnery, however, was miserable. *Cornwallis* fired 30 times without once hitting her adversary. To increase *Hornet*'s speed, Biddle threw overboard his anchors, cable, ammunition, and all his guns but one. After *Cornwallis* stopped firing her guns, she began gaining rapidly on *Hornet* and soon was within range. But only three shots hit *Hornet,* and none of them did any damage. During this action, *Cornwallis* was closer to *Hornet* than *United States* had been to *Macedonian* when she had shot that British frigate to pieces in 1812. While *Cornwallis* was wasting shots, the breeze began to freshen, and *Hornet* started to pull away rapidly. By the next day, the British battleship was 12 miles behind and had to give up the chase.

While *Hornet* was escaping from *Cornwallis, Peacock* headed out alone for the Indian Ocean. She captured four merchant ships carrying valuable cargo and then, on June 30, 1815, hailed the East India Company's war-brig *Nautilus,* which informed *Peacock* that the war was over. Fearing a trick, Warrington answered that if there was peace *Nautilus* should haul down her flag and send a boat over to *Peacock.* When *Nautilus* refused, *Peacock* fired a broadside that wrecked the British ship. Finally, the *Nautilus* convinced Warrington that peace had been made and he released her.

After evading the British blockaders, Captain Stewart had headed *Constitution* for the waters off Spain. On February 20, 1815, she sighted the British heavy corvette *Cyane,* 32 guns, and the sloop-of-war *Levant,* 18 guns. The Royal Navy had ordered its frigates to sail in pairs and never fight an American frigate alone. The *Cyane* and *Levant* were definitely *not* frigates, and their short-range guns could not match the long-range artillery of *Constitution.* But Captain Gordon Falcon of *Cyane* and Captain George Douglass of *Levant* were determined to fight. They did not believe that the navy's order against fighting American ships of superior power applied to them.

The three ships maneuvered while the sun went down and a big moon began riding high in the sky. Firing started at 250 yards, and *Cyane* took heavy punishment while *Constitution* was hardly touched. Smoke now hid the ships, and when it suddenly cleared, *Cyane* and *Levant* were at either end of *Constitution,* ready to sweep her decks with broadsides. In a brilliant maneuver, Captain Stewart actually backed his ship up while pounding both *Cyane* and *Levant* with broadsides. Stewart then swung the lively *Constitution* around the enemy ships, pouring shots into *Cyane* and then *Levant,* which limped off into the darkness. *Constitution* was preparing to sweep *Cyane* with another broadside when she hauled down her flag. The courageous Captain Douglass now brought *Levant* back into action to aid *Cyane,* but the American frigate soon forced her to surrender, too. The two British ships had a total of 92 men killed and wounded. *Constitution* lost only six killed and nine wounded.

Captain Stewart took *Constitution* and the two British warships into the Portuguese city of Porto Praya. He then put his crew to work repairing *Cyane* and *Levant.* On March 10, lookouts reported the approach of three British frigates. These ships, commanded by Admiral Sir George Collier, had been sent out to hunt down the *Constitution.*

Stewart had no faith in the ability of the Portuguese to defend the neutrality of their harbor. Nor did he believe the British would respect Portuguese neutrality. The thing to do was to get out of Porto Praya as quickly as possible. Within 10 minutes, the *Constitution* and her two prize ships, *Cyane* and *Levant,* were under way. *Constitution* easily outran the three British frigates, but *Cyane* began to lag behind. Stewart signaled *Cyane* to leave the other ships and make a run for it. She swung away and, since the British ships did not follow, was able to get to New York in April.

Then *Levant* began to lag, and Stewart ordered her to go off on her own. He believed that the three British frigates would follow the larger ship, *Constitution.* Stewart was astonished when all three frigates took after *Levant.* Admiral Collier lamely explained later that he thought that *Levant* was an American frigate. This would indicate that the admiral did not have very sharp eyes. Later a British naval historian acidly described Collier's action as "the most blundering piece of business recorded in these six volumes."

Hotly pursued, *Levant* managed to scramble back into the harbor of Porto Praya. As Stewart had suspected, the British did not respect the neutrality of the Portuguese city. They moved in and began firing at *Levant*. But, as in the case of *Cornwallis,* the British gunnery was incredibly bad. No shots hit *Levant,* but Porto Praya was practically wrecked. *Levant* finally surrendered, while *Constitution* sailed home to receive the acclaim of the nation. Admiral Collier tried without success to explain his failure to capture *Constitution*. Ten years later, he committed suicide.

20

A NATION UNITED

Before news of Jackson's victory reached Washington, the Federalists had been busy predicting the worst for the nation. Congressman Alexander C. Hanson's newspaper, the *Federal Republican,* said: "The only measure for the preservation of the country which is likely to produce any lasting beneficial results would be the impeachment and punishment of James Madison. While this man, if he deserves the name, is at the head of affairs . . . there can be nothing but dishonor, disappointment and disaster. . . . Turn your eyes to New Orleans. . . . The same contemptable force that retired before the Maryland militia at Baltimore, with the addition perhaps of a few black regiments, are about to cut off, at one slice, a whole state from the union."

Rumors circulated that Jackson was ill and that his troops were short of ammunition. Another Federalist congressman said the British had already taken New Orleans, but that the government was holding back the bad news.

Victory at New Orleans set the whole country to celebrating, and final ratification of the peace treaty kept the celebration going. Grumpy Federalists continued to talk of "Mr. Madison's war" as a useless conflict and a defeat for the United States. But in standing alone in 1814 against Britain, the United States had won worldwide acclaim. For example, Louis Serurier, the French ambassador to the United States, predicted that the war would make the United States a great naval and manufacturing power.

President Madison spoke to all Americans when he said: "If our first struggle [the Revolutionary War] was a war of our infancy, this last was that of our youth; and the issue of both, wisely improved, may long postpone, if not forever prevent, a necessity for exerting the strength of our manhood."

American historian Samuel Flagg Bemis says that the nation experienced that surge of self-respect that a person feels when he finally turns on a bully and fights him. In this case, it was the determination to fight, rather than the outcome, that was important.

Albert Gallatin, who had helped to negotiate the peace with Britain, believed that the war "renewed and reinstated the national feelings which the Revolution had given and were daily lessened. . . . The people . . . are more American; they feel and act more like a nation."

The war also won for America the grudging admiration of some of the most anti-American Britons. Their viewpoint was well expressed by Michael Scott, who lived in Jamaica from 1806 to 1817. Writing in *Blackwood's Magazine,* an English periodical, in 1829, Scott said: "I don't like Americans. I never did and never shall like them. I have seldom met an American gentleman in the large and complete sense of the term. I have no wish to eat with them, drink with them, deal with or consort with them in any way, but let me tell the whole truth—*nor* fight with them, were it not for the laurels to be acquired by overcoming an enemy so brave, determined and alert, and in every way so worthy of one's steel as they have always proved.

"In the field, or grappling in mortal combat on the blood-slippery quarterdeck of an enemy's vessel, a British soldier or sailor is the bravest of the brave. No soldier or sailor of any country, saving and excepting those damned Yankees, can stand against them."

Shortly after the war ended, Winfield Scott visited London and was entertained by General Riall. Forty years later, Scott learned that Sir John M. Wilson, one of Riall's officers at Lundy's Lane, had suffered heavy financial losses when Mississippi failed to pay interest on bonds that Wilson owned. Scott appealed to generous Americans to make up the loss "upon knowledge that the statements of Sir Phineas Riall and Sir John Moryllion Wilson, on their return home, contributed not a little to the liberal final instructions given to the British commissioners who signed the Treaty of Ghent."

21

COMMANDING GENERAL

At the end of the war, President Madison appointed Major Generals Jacob Brown and Andrew Jackson commanders of the peacetime army. Brown would command the northern division and Jackson the southern. The President also appointed Brigadier Generals Scott, Macomb, Ripley, and Gaines to serve with Brown and Jackson on a general board to reorganize the army and recommend which officers were to be retained in the smaller peacetime force.

The peacetime army was cut to 10,000 men, not counting the Corps of Engineers. Only those officers who had served in the war were considered for commissions, and preference was given to graduates of the U.S. Military Academy at West Point. In cutting the number of infantry regiments down to eight, the War Department abolished regiments that had proud records of service. For example, the 9th, 11th, 21st, 22nd, and 25th Regiments, which won fame under General Brown in the Niagara campaign, were absorbed by the 2nd, 5th, and 6th Regiments.

In a few years, Congress became even less generous

toward the army. Republican congressmen saw no reason during peacetime for what they felt was a large regular army. In 1820 Secretary of War John C. Calhoun was ordered to cut the army down to 6,000 men. Calhoun, a member of the fiery War Hawks during the war, had been appointed secretary of war by President Monroe in 1817. He was determined to build a strong regular army, and was quick to resist the attack on it. In a message to Congress, Calhoun argued that if the army was to be cut in size, the reduction should be planned so that it could be expanded quickly in time of war. He said that the experience during the War of 1812 had proved that the regular army, not the militia, could be depended on in a crisis. "I am aware," he added, "that the militia is considered, and in many respects justly, as the great national force; but, to render them effective, every experienced officer must acknowledge that they require the aid of regular troops. . . . War is an art, to attain perfection in which, much time and experience, particularly for the officers, are necessary."

Calhoun proposed to keep a large number of officers in the smaller army while cutting down the number of men in the infantry and artillery companies. Then, in time of war, the companies could be brought up to full strength by adding recruits to them. There would, however, be enough trained officers and men in each company to instruct the recruits and give them confidence when they went into action. But Congress ignored Calhoun's recommendations. It slashed the army to less than 6,000 men and did not adopt his plan for expanding it quickly in time of war.

Although his design for a flexible army was defeated, Calhoun did much to strengthen the War Department and make it more efficient. The beginnings of a general staff of officers to advise and assist the secretary of war had appeared during the War of 1812. Calhoun quickly expanded it and added a commissary general of subsistence to handle the job of feeding the troops, plus a surgeon general and a quartermaster general. The quartermaster general was Thomas S. Jesup, who had won honors at Chippewa and Lundy's Lane and was a longtime admirer of General Brown.

In strengthening the general staff and taking firmer control of the army, Calhoun soon ran into trouble with that rough-and-tumble fighter, General Jackson. The commander of the army's southern division was jealous of his powers and in no mood to take orders from a civilian in Washington. He insisted that he would ignore any War Department orders that tended to "strike at the . . . discipline of the Army." Jackson's clash with Calhoun became so violent that President Monroe had to step in. He told Jackson that the orders of the War Department were the orders of the President, who was commander in chief of the nation's armed forces.

Jackson's invasion of Spanish-held Florida in 1818 aroused not only Calhoun but Congress, Britain, and Spain. When two British adventurers named Arbuthnot and Armbrister stirred up the Seminole Indians against American settlers, Jackson went into action without waiting for government approval. He defeated the Seminoles, invaded Florida, and captured, court-martialed, and hung Arbuthnot and Armbrister. Later, Jackson marched on to Pensacola, kicked out the Spanish governor, and claimed Florida for the United States.

For Jackson's disregard of the chain of command, Calhoun wanted him either court-martialed or at least reprimanded. But Secretary of State John Quincy Adams argued that Jackson had a right to act because the Spanish had not maintained order in their territory. Adams won the argument and Jackson was not punished. Then, Britain denounced Jackson for hanging Arbuthnot and Armbrister, and British newspapers demanded an apology or war. But the British foreign minister, Lord Castlereagh, studied all the facts and decided that Arbuthnot and Armbrister had acted illegally and had gotten what they deserved. Jackson's invasion of Florida convinced the Spanish that they should sell the territory to the United States before that nation took it.

A few years later, in 1821, Jackson retired from the army to become governor of Florida. Calhoun relaxed a bit and took a step he long had considered. He gave the army a single commanding general and brought General Jacob Brown to Washington to fill that post.

During the war, Brown had proven that he could be combative on the field of battle and harsh in his judgment of officers who failed to do their duty. But, unlike Jackson, Brown avoided quarrels with Calhoun. He had quickly recognized that the secretary of war wanted to build a strong army and worked quietly with him for that purpose. As commanding general, Brown continued to cooperate with Calhoun.

Calhoun saw the Military Academy at West Point as an important part of his program to strengthen the army by giving it well-trained leaders. Before the War of 1812, the Academy was in danger of being abolished as unnecessary and expensive. But the excellent performance of West Point graduates during the war won the Academy support from Congress.

West Point also received the wholehearted support of General Brown. In 1815, Brown had been a member of the Military Academy's first Board of Visitors, which consisted of distinguished government leaders, educators, and officers. They studied the Academy and suggested ways that it might be improved. A year later, Brown built, at his own expense, a monument at West Point honoring the brilliant young engineer, Colonel Eleazar D. Wood, who was killed at Fort Erie. Speaking of Wood, Brown said he had "died as he had lived, without a feeling but for the honor of his country and the glory of her arms. His name and example will live to guide the soldier in the path of duty so long as true heroism is held in estimation." Although he had no formal military training, Brown respected the officers from West Point and had been quick to call on their services during the war.

During the years of Brown's service as commanding general, he was disturbed by a quarrel between his two friends Generals Scott and Gaines over who outranked the other. Their rank as brigadier generals bore the same date, but Gaines's name had always led Scott's on the Army Register. The dispute became so hot that Scott challenged Gaines to a duel. Gaines declined, quoting Scott's own regulation against dueling. An outspoken man with a notably touchy temper, Scott was famous for his many quarrels with officers, but he never had a serious disagreement with Brown.

Reviewing the many clashes between secretaries of war and commanding generals of the army, Leonard D. White wrote in his book, *The Jacksonians:* "It could not be said at any time from 1829 to 1861 that the War Department and the Army comprised such a team as that which Calhoun had constructed when he was Secretary of War. These eight years [1817–1825] remained as the epitome of good relations between the Secretary of War, the General Staff and the Army." This era of good feeling and cooperation was due to the quiet work of General Brown as well as that of Calhoun.

During Brown's final years as commanding general, the army's value and that of the Military Academy were strongly questioned again. Many members of Congress echoed the old argument that the nation should put its main trust in a strong militia. They recalled the victory of untrained riflemen at New Orleans and quoted this statement by Andrew Jackson: "Reasoning always from false principles, [the British] expected little opposition from men whose officers even were not in uniform, who were ignorant of the rules of dress, and who had never been caned into discipline. Fatal mistake! A fire incessantly kept up, directed with calmness and unerring aim, strewed the field with the brave officers and men of the [British] column, which slowly advanced, according to the most approved rules of European tactics, and was cut down by the untutored courage of the American militia."

Those who celebrated the militia victory at New Orleans did not choose, however, to quote another statement Jackson had made shortly after that battle ended: "The nature of the troops under my command," he said, "mostly militia, rendered it too hazardous to attempt offensive movements in an open country against a numerous and well disciplined army." General Brown, on the other hand, had led untrained militia against *entrenched* Scots Highlanders at Fort Erie and had made them retreat.

But in spite of Brown's remarkable performance with militia, foes of the army and the Military Academy got no support from the commanding general. Brown did not consider the Fort Erie sortie by militia a strong argument against a well-trained regular army. He had seen what the regulars trained by Scott had done at Chippewa and Lundy's Lane. And the monument he had built at West Point honoring Colonel Wood expressed his feelings about the value of the Military Academy.

Brown's life was shortened by the aftereffects of his Lundy's Lane wound and by a recurring fever he first contracted during the fighting at Fort Erie. He died on February 24, 1828, at the age of 52, and was buried in the Congressional Cemetery in Washington, D.C.

Among the many tributes paid Brown was one from the Marquis de Lafayette. In a letter to Brown's widow he said: "You know, dear madam, the intimate and confidential friendship that had formed between us. Our personal acquaintance was recent . . . but no old intimacy could be more affectionate, no mutual confidence better established."

Secretary of War James Barbour, announcing the death

of Brown, declared: "To say he was one of the men who have rendered most important service to his country would fall far short of the tribute due his character. . . . Quick to perceive, sagacious to anticipate, prompt to decide and daring in execution, he was born with the qualities which constitute a great commander.

"His knowledge of men and his capacity to control them were known to all his companions in arms, and commanded their respect; while the gentleness of his disposition, the courtesy of his deportment, his scrupulous regard for their rights, his constant attention to their wants, and his affectionate attachment to their persons, universally won their hearts, and bound them to him as a father."

All of these words of praise add up to the fact that Brown, the headlong fighter, was one of the greatest battle leaders in America's history. In his chapter on Brown in the book *Eleven Generals,* Fletcher Pratt wrote that "there was some secret of leadership in Brown's presence and manner that made green country boys fight like the devil, and it would be worth a good deal to know that secret. . . . But his secret was the secret of all great leaders, and what man can discover that?"

BOOKS FOR FURTHER READING

Adams, Henry. *The Formative Years*. 2 vols. Boston, Houghton Mifflin, 1947.

————. *The War of 1812*. Edited by H. A. DeWeerd. Washington, published by *Infantry Journal*, 1944.

Beirne, F. F. *The War of 1812*. New York, E. P. Dutton, 1949.

Coles, Harry L. *War of 1812*. Chicago, University of Chicago Press, 1965.

Jacobs, James R. *Tarnished Warrior*. New York, Macmillan, 1938. (Life of James Wilkinson)

Lossing, Benson J. *Pictorial Field Book of the War of 1812*. New York, Harper Brothers, 1869.

Pratt, Fletcher. *Preble's Boys*. New York, William Sloane Assoc., 1950.

Swanson, Neil H. *The Perilous Fight*. New York, Farrar and Rinehart, 1945.

Tucker, Glenn. *Poltroons and Patriots*. 2 vols. Indianapolis, Bobbs-Merrill, 1954.

Weigley, Russell F. *History of the U.S. Army*. New York, Macmillan, 1966.

Index